LIGHTS, CAMERA, REAL ESTATE

SELL MORE REAL ESTATE USING SMARTPHONE VIDEOGRAPHY AND SOCIAL MEDIA STRATEGY

Tracy Ramsay, M.A., Realtor® & Brie E. Anderson
Video Estate Agent, LLC Wichita, KS

Video Estate Agent, LLC
Tracy Ramsay, M.A., Realtor® & Brie E. Anderson

Printed in the United States of America
First Printing 2020
First Edition 2020

978-1-17352888-1-9

LIGHTS, CAMERA, REAL ESTATE

Acknowledgments

We would like to thank Cindy Carnahan and The Carnahan Group, ReeceNichols South Central Kansas for hosting us and being willing to ask questions. We would also like to give special thanks to Kathy Rosell and Katie Brown for being our first participants and favorite guinea pigs. And we extend our most sincere gratitude to Kari Hegstrom who painstakingly read and tried every step-by-step page, ensuring that even the technologically challenged could create professional videos.

We'd also like to thank friends and family who cheered us on even when we were ignoring them, chatting their ears off, or making them listen to us practice (especially in quarantine) - WE LOVE YOU!

Table of Contents

Preface

Gen X Meets Millennial

I'm Tracy Ramsay, a Realtor® with more than twenty years of experience in buying and selling

homes. I had just started working with Brie Anderson, a social media expert, and a member of

the generation born after mine. We were in the middle of preparing a training class together when I brought up what could have been a strain on our very new working relationship.

I looked up at Brie for a moment and then I asked her my burning question, "Do you always wear your baseball hat backward?"

"Yeah," she replied.

"Okay, this is going to be uncomfortable," I said, "but would you consider not wearing it for this training?"

Complete silence. Awkward silence.

Then, thankfully, I heard a slight giggle in her voice, "Do you think if I take my baseball hat off it will increase my subject knowledge?"

Point taken. I tried to explain, "Well, the people taking this class are Realtors® and they dress professionally..."

"That's great," she exclaimed, "I won't ask them to wear backward baseball hats!"

That was the beginning, and end, of our conversation about Brie's backward baseball hat. She was, after all, a Social Media Strategist, consultant to Fortune 500 companies, and the Department Chair of the Digital Media Program at our local college.

She had credentials. She was also bubbly and fun, and I would just pray that the agents would overlook her hat.

I started in real estate by buying and flipping houses in my late twenties. I loved real estate so much that I earned my real estate license and started selling before I was thirty. Spending seventeen blissful years in Duluth Minnesota, I quickly became a top-producing real estate agent. I truly loved my work and had a big book of clients who regularly referred me to their kids, parents, grandparents, friends, and co-workers. Other than wishing my clients "Happy Birthday" or liking a post on Facebook, I never recorded a video or used social media for business, yet it remained on my "someday" list.

One day, my husband decided he wanted to advance in his career, which required us to move out of state—a move I never wanted or anticipated. I begrudgingly left my twenty-year book of business and beloved clients, and moved twelve hours away. I was lucky enough to be invited onto the number one real estate team in Wichita, Kansas, The Carnahan Group, Reece Nichols South Central Kansas, to serve as their sales/accountability coach.

I enjoyed working with the agents on their marketing and sales numbers. But the same theme kept emerging, "We don't want to do social media and video, but know we need to." I didn't blame them, but wasn't very helpful in that arena as I had spent years avoiding it myself. I began feeling desperate to do my part in guiding the agents to resources.

I saw an ad on Facebook that our local college was offering a degree in Digital Marketing. While I wasn't seeking a degree, I thought I owed it to the team to see if I could learn anything new and bring value in this area. I took a class from Brie and was blown away when she taught us how, in 2022, video will make up more than eighty-two percent of online content. That was the push I needed.

Meeting Brie through this class, I had an idea. I asked her if she could train the agents on how to do videos. She said she could teach them everything there was about video and video marketing, but said she knew nothing about real estate, she'd never even bought a house. With both of us bringing our own area of expertise, we decided we could do the training together.

We met outside of class and started designing the training. Two weeks later, the pandemic hit. Videos were no longer a fun, "someday" project, they were a "must do immediately" project. We spent the first thirty days of the pandemic working tirelessly, writing instructions, and training videos for the team. I would tell her what was important in real estate marketing and she would tailor her knowledge and skills accordingly. The result was more than just agent training. We came out with this book and a Blueprint to Video Success. Lights, camera, action, indeed!

Just as Brie and I have bridged our generational gap, we truly hope that this book will bridge your knowledge gap of video to your expertise in real estate, bringing your business quickly into the digital and video age.

Chapter 1

Why Video

Real estate is changing in ways few of us could predict, and most of us could never have imagined. In order to stay ahead of the curve, real estate professionals need to embrace one vital component of our increasingly-digital world: original video content.

When real estate agents are asked the question, "What do you do?" most simply reply, "I sell houses." But is that really all there is to it? Yes, real estate agents *are* in the business of selling homes, but in order to do that, we must first have *clients*. This means attracting and meeting new people, getting to know them, and getting them to not only like you, but trust you with one of the biggest financial and emotional decisions of their life.

In order to sell a house, you must first sell *YOU* to your clients.

The real answer to the question, then, is not that you sell houses, but that you sell *yourself.* Now, when we first start in the real estate business, we are told to call and write letters to everyone we know, everyone our Mom knows, and everyone we've ever met to share the news—I am now in the business of selling houses. We are told to join boards, volunteer for service organizations, and meet as many people as we can for coffee - all in the hopes of finding enough potential clients to know, like, and trust us with their real estate decisions.

Now, while those are all fine practices, you'll need to add one more item to your to-do list: build a video library. After all, by doing this, you make it much easier for all of those family members, friends, and friends of friends to find you and get to know you. Not only do video libraries have the potential to enhance your business model dramatically, but they have become an essential tool in our new digital – and sometimes virtual – world.

At the end of the day, buying and selling houses is no easy feat. After all, few people are eager to entrust a complete stranger with such a monumental decision. However, video allows you to accomplish something that all those Facebook and email messages cannot – conquer anonymity. Simply by going the extra mile with your video content, you can make current and prospective clients alike feel as if you're speaking directly to them, providing them with expert information, and showing them you really care.

When done properly, this alone is often enough to set you apart from the competition.

What's more, if you follow the steps outlined in this book, we promise that the clients who watch your videos will instantly find you more confident, knowledgeable, and trustworthy. With video marketing, you can effectively position yourself as their personal real estate expert, long before you ever meet them.

Why Video?

Video receives 403% more engagement than other mediums of marketing in real estate.[1] From Facebook Live and YouTube to Instagram Live and TikTok, the internet is absolutely chock full of videos. Moreover, social video posts get 1,200% more shares than text posts and images combined,[2] and Facebook video posts are 135% more effective than photos.[3]

Ultimately, there's no escaping the fact that videos help us make decisions more easily. They also keep us informed by showing, not just telling us what we want to know. Currently, nearly five billion videos are watched around the world every single day, with experts estimating that while "consumer video traffic is around 80% of all consumer internet traffic, that number does not even account for videos exchanged peer-to-peer (P2P)." [4]

Put simply, many people just prefer watching videos to reading. This is largely because reading is an active process, while watching is passive. This means that by embracing the potential of videos, you can give your clients the information they want and need without requiring them to do any extra work. After all, life is busy enough! If you can make your clients' lives easier by providing informative videos answering frequently asked questions, they'll reward you with their attention. At the same time, sharing your video content gives your clients a much-needed sense of control, as they get to decide when, what, where, and how much information they need. And, as many of us know, when clients feel in control of a situation, they are far more likely to want to do business with you.

Video content also helps give you a leg up when it comes to website rankings. For instance, did you know that YouTube, with two billion monthly users, is actually the second most popular search engine in the world? And do you know who happens to own YouTube? The first most popular search engine – Google.

It's important to note that Google is partial to both mobile versions of content as well as video content. Moreover, as the undisputed king of all search engines, how your website ranks on Google is extremely important to your ability to marketing strategy. Of course, the more easy-to-access, topic-relevant videos you have on your website, the better your rankings will likely be.

Through the use of keywords, SEO (Search Engine Optimization), and the best possible video uploading and placement, your website can gain valuable attention, which can help your website perform better in search rankings. The better your rankings, the more likely you'll be to turn up in search results, which allows more new customers to find you.

So you see, video content, as well as optimal website rankings, is key to ensuring clients find you before they find your competition.

Luckily, the ease with which videos can be created has allowed the medium to grow exponentially. And because it is so much easier to watch a video rather than read a long description, more and more people are choosing to consume their information this way. Just like in the pre-digital days, catching and keeping attention is what matters. The digital revolution has merely changed the *way* we pay attention and where we choose to focus it. In a world full of distractions and things to see, hear, and do, we don't have enough time to accomplish it all. Video solves this problem by ensuring all your clients have to do is hit "play."

Now more than ever, seeing is believing. With video, clients get to see for themselves what kind of Realtor® you are or explore the houses they might want to purchase more easily. Videos don't just make it easier to make informed decisions - they make it easier to pay attention!

Why Video for Realtors®?

According to the National Association of Realtors®, 98% of all buyers use the internet when shopping for a home.[5] In fact, an increasing amount of new buyers prefer to shop for homes from the comfort of their own living room or from their phone during their lunch break - some people won't even schedule a showing until after they've seen detailed photos of the home's interior.

Statistics also show that homes listed alongside video content get a much higher number of inquiries than those listed without photos or text alone. At the same time, emails that contain videos are 75% more likely to get clients to click through to your listings than just text or images alone, and clients are less likely to opt-out as well.[6] Why? Because people want to get a feel for the homes they're considering. They want to explore the layout, the spaces and rooms, and even the neighborhood. This can't be done merely by looking at photos or reading a description – videos bring homes to life!

Moreover, videos can help you put a face to your business. They allow customers to get to know you (or at least feel that they know you) long before they decide to work with you. Can they trust you? Are you knowledgeable? Making a video helps you tell potential clients who are you and why they should choose you over the competition. In the end, they are more likely to trust a video of you introducing yourself or a video of a happy client than a few sales-oriented paragraphs.

Another benefit to using video content is that it saves you tons of time. Once you make a video, it's made, and you never have to do it again. This means that you can post or add links to relevant videos without having to repeat something you've already explained in that video. Each one can also be placed, viewed, and shared on multiple platforms 24/7. Your videos are working for you all the time!

Here are some compelling facts about the benefits of posting even a single video per week:

Homes listed with videos get four times more inquiries than homes listed without video.[7]

85% of buyers and sellers prefer to work with an agent who uses video marketing techniques.[8]

75% of homeowners are more likely to list with an agent who uses video marketing.[9]

40% of Realtors® have seen an increase of over 40% in profits from the use of video marketing.[10]

The Future is Now

Many of the agents we have worked with are aware that video is an option for marketing their homes and their businesses. However, as an industry, we've all suddenly arrived at a point where video is no longer just *an* option, but often our *only* option.

At the start of 2020, the COVID-19 pandemic turned our world upside down, forever changing the way we would sell property. "Business as usual" no longer existed anywhere, but this was especially true for the real estate community, who had to navigate a new normal in unprecedented times. As an industry where professionals rely heavily on their ability to form intimate relationships with clients, Realtors® were forced to look for other ways to keep their businesses afloat.

While some Realtors® had already caught on to the video trend, many were still in the dark. Almost overnight, in-person showings were replaced with video tours, meetings were being conducted via phone calls or video chats, and anything that required a signature had to be done virtually. All of these previously intimate processes were now being done with some degree of separation, leaving many Realtors® unsure of how to cope.

Of course, not every attempt at a virtual tour or meeting was perfect. Far from it, actually. However, video allowed us to stay connected at a time when being in close proximity to someone could have fatal results. As the months continued and the world slowly started to regain some sense of normalcy, the features and benefits of video highlighted by the pandemic proved far too effective to leave behind.

As a real estate marketing tool, video has been an option for quite some time, but it took a pandemic to prove its true value. This presents all of us with a huge opportunity. Rather than wait for the next disaster to strike, we can start embracing video content now. Luckily, producing video content has never been easier. Moreover, the longer you wait to embrace the technology, the more you miss out on the benefits!

In this book, you will learn everything you need to know about how to make videos that work for your business. From production to marketing, we'll show you how we can take our entire industry to the next level.

Chapter 2

Produced, Personalized, and Live Video

By learning the differences between produced, personalized, and live video, and when and how you use them, you'll start creating a library of good content for now and into the future.

In our current marketplace, there are three types of videos: produced, personalized, and live. Each of these videos serves a different purpose and they each also require different tools. It is important that when you start working on your video library you understand the purpose of each, and how they will fit into your larger video strategy.

In marketing, they say it takes seven touchpoints to get a potential client to take action. In real estate, an action may be the request for a viewing, or it may be the purchase of the house. The touchpoints you use to get someone to take the action of calling you to look at a house are different than the touchpoints needed for getting them to purchase it. Either way, you can use videos to get you closer to your specific goal. It's never too early to get in front of a homebuyer to start building trust and showing expertise.

Produced Video

Produced videos are the kind of video you are most likely used to seeing. "Produced" means just that—it takes a lot of production to create them. They require a hired videographer, hours of shooting with sets, top-of-the-line equipment and hours of post-production work. We see produced videos in real estate for virtual tours or open houses.

These are extremely professional videos and take a lot of time (and money) to create.

While often quite impressive, these videos are not that personal. When it comes to marketing, these videos are considered "top-of-funnel," meaning the viewers are still pretty far from converting, or buying, the house. Produced video requires very little buy-in from the viewer and does little to build trust in the listing agent. Produced videos can be used to showcase a product or for very formal communication, such as commercials.

In this book, we are going to focus on personalized and live videos—where you have the greatest opportunity for growing your personal brand and for helping your clients take those actions to ultimately buy or sell a house.

Personalized Video

Personalized videos are the videos you take, but it doesn't mean they aren't well produced. They serve a very different purpose than the produced videos discussed previously. There are multiple types of personalized videos ranging from evergreen to timely. They all require smart planning, strategy, and quality production. We will be going over these in greater depth later in the book.

Personalized videos are valuable for one obvious reason—they're your bridge to showing what only you can bring your clients: your personality, your charm, your empathy ... everything we pick up on when we meet someone face-to-face. This is the time for YOU to shine. When you don't have the opportunity to get in front of the potential buyer in person, then personalized video will allow you to build trust in a virtual but meaningful way.

Through personalized video, your potential homebuyer can get to know you, your mannerisms, and how you carry yourself—these are all the things that endear us to other human beings. As stated earlier, video allows you to display nonverbal cues, many of which are key when it comes to building trust.

Personalized Video Categories

There are two major categories of personalized videos Realtors® should focus on: evergreen and timely.

The overall goal of this book is to help you create a video library that you can access whenever you need it. The more diversified types of videos you have stored means that many more tools in your virtual toolbox whenever you need them. One of the most obvious categories of video we want to fill is **evergreen** content. Evergreen content is content that is relevant forever (or just for a long time). These videos include answers to common questions, introductions, tips, and tricks.

The second type are **timely videos** which are relevant to a specific time period. In today's environment, a timely video may be "How to Show Your House While Social Distancing." Timely videos can also be videos that are related to some sort of trend like the Lip Sync Challenge that was popular for a few years on late night shows. Last year's timely video might be water bucket challenges, next year's might be influenced by TikTok songs. Other timely videos might be a mix of evergreen *and* timely, like "Moving in the Middle of School Sessions."

Timely videos might also be market-driven. Videos you take showcasing your new listings are considered timely. Another example could be a new home development in a specific neighborhood in your area. This boom time may only be relevant for a short time, but if you make a timely video of market trends in a hot neighborhood, your credibility will be noticed by potential clients who are looking to you as the expert in housing fluxuations. While these videos may only be relevant for a short period of time, they are extremely engaging and effective at drawing attention.

Live Video

Live video is reserved for one very specific moment in time. Live videos should only be used when you are willing and able to interact with the audience. If you have no intention of interacting with the audience, then live video is not the right avenue.

Live video is the ultimate connector as it is the closest thing we can get to having an in-person conversation online. Sometimes, live video is one-to-many, on platforms like Facebook Live, Instagram Live, or YouTube Live. Sometimes, live video can be one-to-one on platforms like FaceTime or Zoom.

These live videos are extremely helpful after your initial meeting or conversation with clients when they have more clarifying questions. While many of us are used to doing business via phone calls, video calls can be far more personal and helpful when it comes to conversations intended to further cement working relationships. Again, this comes back to selling yourself and building trust

Chapter 3

Your Content Strategy

Learn how to write content for the personalized and live videos you'll need to build your winning real estate video library.

Just as you've accepted your new role as videographer, now you have to be a screenwriter, too? On the surface this part can feel intimidating. Negative thoughts may creep into your mind such as, "I don't like my voice" or "what if I say the wrong thing?" I don't know anyone who likes to hear their own voice, but after decades of speaking the same way, you aren't going to change it, so you may as well accept it. As far as making a mistake, you can always do a retake. Imperfect is sometimes perfect, it's entirely human and endears people to you, which can lead to trust. Don't be afraid to be creative and to be yourself in your videos.

Coming up with content and recording videos is similar to giving a speech or doing a sales presentation which, as Realtors®, you do all the time. You most likely give the same mini-speech every time you go over a purchase agreement with a buyer, or when you present an offer to a seller. You'll be doing the same thing in the videos you'll be recording.

There are some people who can take any topic, sit comfortably in front of a camera, speak naturally, and deliver a perfect video on the first take. And then there are the rest of us. If you are one of those blessed people who can speak extemporaneously with little or no preparation, consider yourself lucky. But if you are like the majority of the population, you need a plan. This next section will help you plan and write your video content.

Know Your Audience - Creating a Persona

In real estate, you are marketing to past, present, and future buyers or sellers, as well as their referral sources. It is important to know who your target audience is for each video. This will help you stay focused on how to best present the material. Video scripts should be well-informed but personable. They should be you talking to whoever is watching the video. Your viewers should feel a connection to the speaker.

One way to help you achieve this is to create a persona (for a buyer and a seller). A persona is a semi-fictional representation of the client(s) or audience you are marketing to. In real estate, some examples would be first-time home buyers, retirees, families with children, or military personnel. The purpose in creating a persona is to help you stay on track and personalize your message. It also gives you "someone" to talk to while you are recording the video.

Large companies use personas regularly in marketing. They will often name their persona and make an avatar of them to refer to as they direct their marketing. They do extensive research tracking their potential client's age, sex, location, income, education level, familial status, ethnicity, occupation/profession, habits, personality, spending habits, motivations, hobbies, and preferred channels of communication. Some industries add additional criteria. For instance, in real estate, you can include real estate experience and real estate needs.

Marketing companies do extensive research and spend tens of thousands of dollars coming up with their personas. You don't need to do that. You can create your persona by looking at the demographics of either your past clients or clients you want to attract.

Here is an example of a real estate persona:

Sally the seller/buyer: Age 55, married, middle class, three grown children, one grandchild, soon-to-be retired teacher, loves gardening, has lived in her current house for twenty-five years, looking to downsize to a townhouse.

With this persona top of mind, there are a number of videos that might appeal to Sally. Because she wants to sell her home of twenty-five years, try a video on "Staging Your House to Sell." Sally loves gardening, so add a tip about having fresh cut flowers on the table. Because Sally is also looking to buy a townhouse, create videos to help her with this purchase, like what to consider in an HOA when buying a home. Or, perhaps a video highlighting a new townhome development in your area.

Here's a template that will help you create your own persona. It can be downloaded at https://videoestateagent.com/book-downloadables/ and use the password: MoreViews. For a more in-depth persona, go to www.realestatepersonabuilder.com.

PERSONA TEMPLATE

Persona:

Name:

Gender:

Age:

Profession:

Familial status:

Hobbies:

Current living situation:

Past real estate experience:

Real estate aspirations:

Any concerns/worries/questions:

Writing content

Once you've decided who your audience is for a particular video, you want to follow this simple format for every video:

- Introduce yourself and your company.
- Introduce the topic: Make it interesting, grab their attention.
- Give substance: Make it worth their time with quality information.
- Outro: Use a memorable closing statement. Thank them for viewing.
- Call to action: Tell the viewers how to reach you and request that they like, share, and subscribe.

Ten tips to help you write authentic, captivating video content:

1. Know your audience.
2. Determine your goal for the video.
3. Determine a clear takeaway for your viewers. What do you want them to learn?
4. Write a clear and specific Call to Action. What do you want viewers to *do* after they watch?
5. Be authentic. Viewers can feel when you are being phony.
6. Introduce yourself and the topic. If you are including another person in the video, a loan officer or property inspector for instance, decide beforehand who will be doing the primary speaking in the video.
7. Write conversationally. When you write to your target audience, you should envision that you are speaking directly to your audience through the camera.

8. Be concise but thorough. People prefer shorter, entertaining videos.
9. Focus on keeping transitions natural, like they would in a conversation. Plan for transitions in your script so you are ready for them when you run through the script.
10. Keep good notes. The better the notes, the easier this will be when you start recording.

Should you use a script?

While you don't want to sound "scripted," you should at least take the time to write down your key points. The more detailed you are in your written script, the easier it will be when it comes time to record your video. The key to writing a script is to be thorough with your notes. For example, if you later intend to include video clips or photographs or charts in the video about a specific neighborhood, make a note to address it like you would talking, "you can see here that the Belltown neighborhood is a fun, busy place after eight p.m." This keeps content seamless. You can easily mark these parts in your script with bold or in all-caps "CLIP OF BELLTOWN—35 seconds—name off the various hotspots" so you know when going over the script you'll have thirty-five seconds to talk about the clip or to add some appropriate music as it happens. We have created a free, downloadable video script template you can use to help you. It can be downloaded at: https://videoestateagent.com/book-downloadables/.

VIDEO SCRIPT TEMPLATE

Introduction

Topic & Purpose

What you want them to know

Conclusion

Call to Action

Finally, don't be afraid to try new things. If you are still unsure what kind of scripts will feel most natural to you, think about the videos you like. Think about the commercials you like, and ask yourself why? What is it about these videos and commercials that makes you like them?

Three Main Categories of Video Content

Now we're going to learn about the three main categories of video content: educational, awareness, and engagement. Some of the examples can overlap and fall into more than one category.

- **Educational videos**: Informative content is content that helps build your credibility as a real estate professional.
- **Awareness videos**: When you want to grab attention, these are the best kinds of videos to get you on your client's radar. The more fun and entertaining your awareness video (but not ridiculous, inappropriate or over-the-top), the more likely you are to attract new clients.
- **Engagement videos**: When you want to appeal to people's emotions or to get them to interact with your video via likes or comments, these videos are your opportunity to be personable with your clients.

Once you've decided on the purpose of the video, educational, awareness, or engagement, you can explore some different kinds of videos that fall within these three categories.

Educational Videos

Question and Answer (Q&A)

People have questions. You have answers. Make a list of all the questions you've been asked by clients. Even if you are just starting out, you can think of questions you had when buying your home. Then, start making short videos to answer these questions. You can do an interview style Q&A where someone is asking you a question and you respond. Or, you can simply state the question and answer it. This will help save you time in the future. You can even include Q&A videos in emails for quick handling without repetition.

How-to/Explainer

How-to/Explainer videos are like Q&As but are more in-depth. They include topics clients may not even realize they should know. These videos will help build your trust and credibility as a Realtor®. Some examples of good how-to/explainer videos answer these types of questions:

How to save for a down payment

What benefits can I take advantage of as a first-time home buyer?

How to take advantage of Veteran's benefits

Home Inspections 101

Negotiating 101

The sky's the limit with How-to/Explainer videos. The more videos you make and put out there, the more likely someone will stumble upon them, and the more credibility you build in your community as the go-to person for home buying.

Case Study/Testimonial

What better way to convince potential clients you are the best person to help them find their perfect home than by showing them all of the happy people you've already helped? Seeing is believing. Testimonial videos help build confidence through positive experiences. Watching a testimonial video about someone who is happy in their new home can help ease the worry of potential clients. Making a case study video walks a client through the problems that arose for other clients, and how it turned out okay for them in the end. This can build confidence when inevitable hiccups happen in the home buying process. Clients can learn firsthand how it worked out well for another client who experienced a similar issue.

Announcements

Announcements can be anything from a new colleague coming on board to a new listing. Anything exciting and new that you want to share. Announcement videos keep your clients up to date on your business, as well as help build excitement for new benefits they will have access to or even new homes available in their dream neighborhood.

Service Tour

A service tour gives first-time visitors to your site a go-to to find out what services you offer. This video should be concise, but thorough. It is more enticing to watch a short video than to read a lot of text to find out what services you provide. Do you do in-house financing? Do you offer referrals for home inspectors? Are you VA (Veterans Affairs) approved? Do you provide listings for VA-approved homes? Make a list of all the services you provide, then make a service tour video.

Live Talks/Presentations

If you or your colleagues are giving a speech or presentation, record it. This is an easy way to make a video that'll be informative and engaging, allowing viewers to learn more about you and how you handle yourself. You can edit and post it to share it with others who didn't attend your presentation. You could also hold a live Q&A about home buying, about financing, about down payments, about home inspections, etc. These make Q&A videos even more relatable and interesting.

Interviews with Other Professionals

As real estate agents, you understand you can't *and shouldn't* know everything. You rely on other professionals throughout the home selling process, such as loan officers, home inspectors, and insurance agents. If you feature them, they can also share the videos you post on their social media sites and, in return, you get more traffic. It's a win-win!

Awareness Videos

Round-ups

Round-up videos are catchy. They are click-bait like "Five Up and Coming Neighborhoods in Toronto" or "Ten Best Neighborhoods to Raise your Kids in Seattle." These should be short (less than five minutes long) to keep your audience engaged. Make sure to include clips of relevant stats such as school ratings for a neighborhood, crime rates, etc. They should also include visuals: photos of the neighborhoods, passenger side clips driving through them, etc. Your audience will stay interested with a visual taste of the neighborhoods and they can be a game changer for out-of-town buyers.

Make a wide range of these videos; the more you make, the more people you will reach. Take a poll of what is important when buying a house. Get creative, think outside the box. "Five Reasons Single Thirty Somethings Will Love the Green District" or "Ten Outdoor Activities in the Soho District." Make a round-up video for everyone!

Interviews with Clients

Interviews help express your values and align you with people you feel also live your values. Perhaps you sold a house to someone you volunteer with from a service organization you belong to. In their interview they might mention that they chose you as their agent because not only are you great at what you do, but you also care about the community, which is important to them. Or maybe you sold a house to someone relocating to town, they could talk about you being the area expert who goes the extra mile for their clients and makes the relocation process easy. Have you sold a home to someone famous? Someone influential? Interviewing them about why and how they came to choose their home, and why they went with you, can go a long way to helping build your brand.

Behind the Scenes

Behind the Scenes videos can include how you choose the homes you sell, how you decide what is important to list, and most importantly what you do behind the scenes for your clients. Again, this is a place where you can get creative to show the client you want to help them find their perfect home, and all the things you will do to ensure that happens. Have you ever seen the TV show *Fixer Upper* with the adorable couple in Texas who choose three homes to present to their clients, each home with its own issues for their clients to choose one to be remodeled? Each episode is filled with behind-the-scenes footage that keeps viewers interested. You can do something similar. A little creativity will bring your personality to life and can make a difference in how people see you.

Meet the Team/Company Culture

Here's your opportunity to not only introduce yourself, but that fabulous bunch of people you work with who are helping you help your clients. Interview one another or tell viewers why you are the best real estate team who will have their back. What do you offer that others do not? What do you excel at? These kinds of videos help you stand out from your competitors.

Engagement Videos

Vlogs

Vlogs are video blogs where you share a diary-like series of videos on your journey or experience as a Realtor®. Search YouTube for "Real Estate Vlogs" to see examples of popular ones. While there's no strict standard, vlogs are a series of things you want to share with potential/current clients. These might include new listings, standard improvements made before selling homes, bilingual listings, etc. The key to vlogs is to be consistent. If you commit to one post a week, do one post a week on the same day and time every week. Make it something worth waiting for each week. Consistency and creative content are the keys to a successful vlog.

Video Emails

Under a minute long, just enough time to grab a viewer's attention, video emails can be very effective. You only want a short amount of text to encourage the reader to click for more information. They also work as a quick introduction to you, what you can offer, and are an engaging way to greet a client/potential client when you can't meet in person.

Video emails are also a digital segue to arrange a phone call or set up a meeting or a home viewing. You can make a variety of video emails to use again and again with different clients. Keep them simple and short, but personable.

Humorous Skits

Laughter is the soul of connection and a funny video can help clients relate to you. If you can make someone smile, grin, or laugh out loud, you humanize your brand, making it relatable. You could do a skit on how not to sell a home. You could combine a humorous video with a round-up video, "Five Spooky Properties I Would NEVER Try to Sell You" or "How to Butter Up Your Realtor® to Get a Discount." This is another chance to be creative. What would make you laugh? What do you think is funny? Chances are others will find the same things funny as well.

Trends

Trends connect us to the community at large, can be loads of fun and sometimes also fall under the awareness category. Remember the Water Bottle Flip that annoyed all the moms? Or The Git Up Challenge that had everyone dancing? Pour some ice over your broker's head, challenge your kids—or better yet, your client's kids—to a water bottle flip contest, put on your dancing shoes and turn on your video camera! It's fun for your audience to see their Realtor® as trendy, because if you keep up with those trends, then you are most likely keeping up with housing trends, too!

Live Videos

When you are actively engaging live with your audience, it's almost like being in the same room with them. Use the platforms you know and that you expect your clients will use, whether it's FaceTime, Zoom, Facebook Live, Instagram Live or TikTok.

Examples of live videos:

- Virtual open home visits
- Livestream auctions
- Real-time home closings (capture it on video when someone moves in or when they sign their papers, when they choose their house, etc.)

- Show off a neighborhood (drive through it, walk through it, record the highlights live)
- Showcase a local park, coffee shop, art gallery, restaurant, etc.
- Interview someone (staging a home, buying a home, looking for a home, inspecting a home)
- Real-time home inspection
- Discuss the property market with a local specialist
- Tell your success stories
- Broadcast life moments (building rapport and personal relationships with your clients)
- Offer advice to home buyers/sellers on the spot when you think of them (and are camera ready)
- Host contests and giveaways. Get the community involved by giving a gift card to a local restaurant or coffee shop. This builds goodwill all around, and makes people remember you. Bring out your natural performer. Real estate agents are some of the best dressed and attractive people out there! Put that charm and good looks to use! Take the opportunity to go live when you can!

Personalizing Your Videos

Data suggests over fifty percent of consumers want to see more video content from brands they follow. Over ninety percent are more likely to go with brands they recognize, remember, and that can provide relevant recommendations. As a Realtor® *you* are your brand. Helping build your brand will help you gain new clients and keep existing ones.

In the digital era, it is easy to feel like content is thrown at you from every direction. This kind of content doesn't feel particularly personal;

it is often irrelevant and people can easily get turned off by information they didn't ask for. By personalizing your videos, you help your viewers feel like each video was made for them, like the videos you share with them are relevant to them. This will help build trust and confidence in your ability to help them find the right home. They will feel like they matter. Other advantages to using personalized videos include:

- Greater possibility for conversion
- Deeper relationships with your clients
- A better understanding of your target audience
- Improved brand affinity and brand loyalty
- Higher ROI from marketing and advertising
- A shorter and more efficient sales cycle

Examples of personalized videos:

- **Invitations.** Invites to view a home or to attend an informational event can be made more personal by speaking directly to clients. Example, "I have the perfect home for you to see on Saturday... I hope to see you there at ten a.m."

  Send the relevant listings to relevant clients/potential clients. Does a client want a fixer upper? Are they looking for a Craftsman style home? Mention these key things in the video by saying something like, "This is a remodeled 1920s Craftsman, just like you wanted," or "This house is in a great neighborhood, I know how important that is to your family." Find little ways of making the invites stand out and feel personal with specific and relevant details.

- **Holiday Greetings** Warm wishes during celebratory times are an excellent way of staying in contact with people you want to do business with. It is also a way of connecting and creating goodwill. Who doesn't like to be thought of during the holidays? Make it even more personal by sending a specific holiday greeting if you know them well enough.

- **Calls to Action** Asking for the order is the golden rule of sales. Use their name in the video and talk about things they've mentioned are important to them. Consider including graphics or images that are relevant to them. For example, if you know Lisa is looking for a condo near a thriving nightlife area downtown, include photos of clubs and activities within walking distance and then ask her if you can schedule time for a showing.
- **Thank You Videos** Sharing simple messages of gratitude to clients for contacting you, for getting information back on time, for buying a home from you, for referring a friend or family member to you, for anything you would normally say thank you for is a simple, yet powerful way to let them know they matter.

Building Your Library

Optimally, you will make many videos. Some will be relevant for a short period of time. Some will remain relevant and useful over time. The term "evergreen" represents the videos on your website that will always be relevant to your audience, as opposed to those topics that may change over time. Many of these were covered in the Educational, Engagement, and Awareness sections that covered client spotlights, testimonials/case studies, behind-the-scenes, thank yous, about us, Q&As, educational / informational, etc. As you grow your library with various content and get more ideas of your clients' needs, you will come up with new ideas for toolkit videos specific to certain groups such as first-time home buyers or veterans. You can engage with a world issue such as buying a home during quarantine or buying a home when the economy isn't doing great, or reasons to buy a home when you currently rent. Focus on building your evergreen content first, while still creating other new and creative videos along the way.

You can learn more in Chapter 16, Building Your Video Library, with over fifty video ideas, and Chapter 17, Blueprint for Video Success, to get you started. In the next chapter we go over tips to help you talk on camera.

Chapter 4

Talking on Camera

With a few tips and some practice, talking on camera can be fun and easy.

For most people, the thought of speaking into a camera and recording themselves for the whole world to see evokes fear and anxiety. Emotions can run anywhere from butterflies in the stomach to sheer panic. There is actually a term for this, *glossophobia*. But fortunately, there are tips and tricks you can use to help alleviate your fears so you can deliver a smooth video you'll be proud to post.

First, practice, practice, practice. Some people think they can just "wing it" but, in reality, the more you go over your speech, the better you'll do. When you watch a TV show, the actors make it look so easy. But that's because they spend hours going over their scripts, making sure they have the perfect voice inflection and facial expressions.

Smile, be enthusiastic, and friendly. The main purpose of these videos is to sell *you.* As a salesperson, you've already mastered the art of engaging with clients face-to-face. Now you need to bring your award-winning—or at least commission winning—personality to video. Even though it may not feel natural because you are sitting in front of a camera, it's important to act friendly and enthusiastic about your topic. The best way to do that is to start with a warm, genuine smile.

Dress for success. You feel your best when you look your best. Looking your best does not mean wearing a three-piece suit or formal dress, but make sure you dress and prepare yourself so you can feel confident on camera. If you are uncomfortable with your appearance, it will show on camera.

Talk to your persona. In the last chapter we went over how to come up with a persona, the fictional representation of your audience. That is the person you should direct your video to. Some people even tape up a picture or use a cardboard cut-out behind the camera. Try different techniques and see what works best for you. Pretend the camera is your client standing in front of you.

Look into the camera lens. Consider the camera lens as your persona's eyeballs. By looking directly at the camera, you will appear more confident and knowledgeable. It will make your audience feel as if you are speaking directly to them.

Use notes or a teleprompter. Most people tape notes next to the camera or have a big noteboard with bullet points written on it. It's okay to look at your notes, just try not to stare at them too long so it is obvious to viewers.

If notes don't work well for you, you can try using a teleprompter app. A teleprompter app allows you to write, or download your script or notes, and have them scroll across the screen as you record yourself speaking. You still need to practice so it doesn't look like you are reading from a script, but they can be extremely useful, especially if you are recording a longer video. They have useful features that allow you to adjust the size and speed of the text. There are a number of different apps in the App Store or Google Play. Most of them have free downloads with in-app purchases or a one-time fee of around fifteen dollars, which is money well spent if you plan to record a lot of videos.

Now that you know what to say, and how to say it, in the next chapter you will learn how to use equipment that will help you look and sound like a polished professional.

Chapter 5

Using the Right Equipment and Lighting

A small investment in the right tools, and some knowledge of the basics of content, light, and audio, will set the stage for high-quality video production.

The thought of producing, starring in, and editing your own video might feel incredibly intimidating. But, with some basic instructions and thoughtful planning, you will be surprised how even people with zero experience in video *can* make that leap. **All you need to get started is your iPhone/smartphone (**Recommended phones are iPhone 8 or newer and Samsung Galaxy 9 or newer).

For some of you, that may be the only piece of equipment you ever need or use. You don't have to purchase new equipment or necessarily hire an entire production crew. You are going to learn how to use as little equipment as possible to get the very best video possible. With that said, a small investment in additional equipment can go a long way.

Surprisingly, it does not take much to make a professional looking, engaging video. There are three main components to all quality video:

- Content
- Audio
- Lighting

Content

When you are creating a video, you should always start by defining your goal. Think back to the two types of personalized video: Timely and Evergreen. Is your intent to share information that any home seller might want? Or do you hope to share a special message to buyers possibly interested in one specific house?

Once you have a goal in mind, you will have a better sense of what needs to go into your video. For example, let's say you want to create a video to explain the importance of a home inspection to show your expertise. You should know, likely off of the top of your head, four or five things that have to be said in that video to truly *add value* for a potential buyer, and help position you as an expert in the industry.

After you've decided what you are going to say and how you are going to add value, you have to think about the delivery. How are you going to keep people engaged throughout the video? Generally speaking, when working on a personalized video, the video should be between three to five minutes and no longer or you will lose their interest. If you are posting a video on social media, your video should be no longer than ninety seconds.

Keeping people's attention is tough, so you have to find ways to keep your viewers engaged. Whether it's through your inflection or gestures, or if it's adding text and music to the video in post-production, these slight changes re-engage the audience.

Audio

Nobody wants to listen to a video with terrible sound quality. It's unpleasant and hard to follow. That's why audio is one of the first things video creators encourage newcomers to invest in. You would be surprised by the difference even a five dollar plug-in lapel microphone can make in the sound of your video.

Our phones are meant to pick up sound from all directions. When you are in an open room, it is going to be collecting sound from every direction. Let's say you're in the middle of a ten by fourteen-foot room and your phone is three feet in front of you. As you speak, your phone will have no problem picking up the words you are speaking. The issue is that the sound of your voice will also bounce off all of the walls around you, and head back towards the phone. So, whatever is happening in the room, the phone is created to pick up those sounds. All of that sound can create a slight echo (reverb), which is not very easy on the ears.

Microphones, on the other hand, have much less gain, or audio capturing signals, which allow them to pick up far less extra noise. In this same ten by fourteen-foot room, a wireless lapel microphone (a microphone that attaches to your clothing and is attached to a lightweight battery or iPhone by an inconspicuous wire) will help for a few reasons. The first is that it looks the most professional and is the least distracting. The second is that it is created to pick up on the sound directly above it (your voice). And the third is that it allows you to walk around without having to worry about wire plug-ins or sound quality.

Using these microphones with your smartphone is easy, it plugs into the same place your headphones do. You will then connect the microphone's wireless adapter to the one you just plugged into your phone. Once it is plugged in, your phone automatically recognizes that there is a new audio input and starts waiting for that sound to come through.

The only "setting up" you will have to do to start feeding sound to your smartphone is turning on your microphone's two wireless adapters (one connected to your phone, one connected to your microphone).

You always want to double check that your sound is being picked up without echos or other interference by making a few test videos and listening to them. You may not be able to listen to your video with the microphone plugged in, so if you don't hear sound at first, unplug your microphone and play the video again. If you still don't have sound, double check that both parts of your wireless microphone are on. Then, plug your microphone back in and try again.

If you decide to shoot video outdoors, a voiceover in post-production will deliver the best audio quality. This means you shoot the video outdoors, but then make sure to record speech inside in a room set up for quality sound capture. However, if you are going to be talking on camera outdoors, you will have to use that audio as your lips will be moving and if you do a voiceover, you'd have to match the words **exactly** to your lip movements. The best recommendation for recording outdoor speech is to wait until there is no wind, use the wireless microphone, and try not to move around too much. It's realistic to expect that when you record outside, you'll pick up some background noise.

Lighting

Lighting is one of the most important things that will help you make a video look professional. Natural lighting is the best kind of lighting, and you are likely to find a few places in your home or office that will work best for your video. There will be times where natural lighting is not an option, or it may not offer enough coverage to make a good looking video. You'll then need to set up good artificial lighting to replace or supplement any natural lighting.

Smart Tip: Purchase a twelve to eighteen-inch ring light that is mounted on a five to six-foot tripod. This ring light will be perfect for either producing light or complimenting the natural light you have access to.

Lighting Basics

You already have learned that the core of your business is selling *yourself*. A video may be the first time a potential client has ever seen you, so putting your face in the best possible light (pun intended!) is critical to a good first impression.

First ensure the lighting on your face is even and not too harsh or too dark. Put your phone in selfie mode (where you can see yourself in the camera) and start testing different places in the room. You'll quickly start to notice a few things:

Front Lighting

Front lighting is the best kind of lighting. While it may be hard to get used to, having a light directly in your face, that isn't too harsh, is the absolute best kind of lighting for a video.

Back Lighting

If the light source is behind you, you will get a silhouette look where the light is pretty bright, but your face is rather dark in comparison. This look can make it hard for viewers to see your eyes, therefore making it harder for them to connect with you.

- **The Fix.** If you find yourself in a position where the light is behind you, you have a few options. The first is to simply reverse your position and put the light in front of you. However, if you are trying to show off a large window or glass door and that light source *needs* to be in the shot, bring the ring light and place it in front of you to even out the light sources. The last option would be to turn sideways where you can talk about the feature while lighting half of your face naturally and place a ring light opposite the feature to light the other half of your face.

Ceiling Lighting

Light from above can cast hard shadows on the bottom half of your face. The most common source of lighting in houses and offices is from fixtures placed on ceilings. This lighting is not very even, and for some, it can be unflattering.

- **The Fix** The ring light should be able to help with lighting from above. You will want to start by placing the ring light directly in front of you to see if that helps. If not, you may need to lower your ring light in an attempt to even out the lighting. The main goal is not *perfectly even* lighting, instead, a clear shot without too much shadowing.

Side Lighting

Lights from the side do a great job of hiding half of your face, and are a trick used in gritty crime movies and film noir to set an ominous mood. But that's the opposite of what you want to do in real estate! You want to use video to build *trust,* not suspicious characters. Side lighting can happen when you stand in a room and have a window on either side of you, or if there is a lamp on in the room.

- **The Fix.** A few things can be changed pretty easily with side lighting. If you do not need the window open because it is not in the shot, pull the curtain over it to dim some of the lighting. If a lamp needs to be on, try to move it in front of you. If either of these things cannot be changed, pull out your handy ring light and place it on the opposite side of your current light source (window or lamp) which will balance the side light.

Attachable LED Lighting

Another handy tool is an attachable, battery-powered LED light. This light can attach to your tripod or gimbal to ensure direct lighting in your shot. This light is going to be especially useful during videos where you are moving around rather quickly and won't have the time to set up and perfect the lighting for each shot.

Lighting is a skill that will need some trial and error before you get it right, but once you start to figure it out, it comes rather naturally.

Ideally, you would choose your shots based off of the lighting, but there will be times where you have to work in a place with less than ideal lighting and find a way to make it work. It will only take a few of those instances to get the hang of using the tools you have to know how to set yourself up for success regardless of the situation.

Chapter 6

How to Shoot a Quality Video

Learn the basics of shooting a quality video that clients will want to watch.

What to Wear

Let's start with the thing everyone is thinking—what the heck should I wear? To be fair, Brie is very much a millennial who's into wearing jeans and a T-shirt while working in her field, but Tracy has spent years working in real estate and operates under the professional dress-for-your job mantra. The happy medium is what you should aim for when prepping for your video. You don't need to be wearing a little black dress or a high-power business suit as if you were attending an interview at a financial firm. Business casual is more the norm for real estate professionals. The most important dress code to follow is one that matches your personal brand. You are trying to humanize yourself with video, so what you're wearing should be reflective of who you are.

In addition to working within the 'rules' of your real estate dress code, video also calls for a very specific wardrobe. You want to stay away from small patterns at all costs (patterns like gingham or small stripes) as they are hard on the eyes in video. Also, you may not be one hundred percent aware of what your background is going to be for your entire video and you don't want to wear something busy with a lot of different patterns, textures or colors, especially if you're going to have a somewhat busy background.

Think about the color of your setting before choosing your outfit. If you are going to show a listing and all of the walls are blue, don't wear blue. Or, if you are shooting a shot where you'll be sitting in red chairs, red and possibly russets or orange, are not the colors you want to be wearing. For the most part, solid neutrals and dark colors are safe. Anything too bright may make the lighting seem harsh or add an odd reflective glow around your face.

Depending on your editing skills, you may want to create backgrounds by using a green screen. In cases like this, any color green clothing or accessories can cause issues.

Tone down the bling. Oversized jewelry that has a lot of stones that catch the light or create a sparkling look can distract and create streaks or flashes. Keep jewelry simple and try for muted stones and metals.

Setting the Shot in Your Home

Now that you're all dressed and ready to go, you have to find where you are going to shoot. It is best to choose your shot with lighting in mind. However, you may not have too much of a choice with where you need to shoot, and you may just have to fix the lighting once your shot is set.

So, to create your shot, you want to start by looking for a clean background. You don't want anything too terribly distracting behind you such as children playing, cluttered objects, or a very bright-colored wall. YOU are the focus when you are speaking and anything that distracts from you hampers your goal of building trust and selling yourself. Ideally, you would find a clean room, a blank wall or a green screen to be in front of.

Once you know where you are going to be shooting, you should use painter's tape to mark where you will sit or stand. This should be about three feet (an arm's length) away from any large object that the camera could focus on. Then, three feet in front of that mark is where your camera should be set up. This setup will ensure that your camera stays focused on you and not anything behind you. Depending on your camera settings (like portrait mode), the background may even be slightly blurred to keep you in focus.

Making Eye Contact

Now that you know where your camera needs to be, you must set your camera at *your* eye level. Having the camera at eye level will make it easier to look into the camera and therefore "look" into the eyes of your audience. This eye contact is important for building trust, so you will want to make sure you are looking straight at the camera. Some tricks you can use is to have someone stand on the other side of the camera, or to tape a cutout face onto the back of your phone so it feels like you are looking at someone when you speak.

The other upside to having your camera stabilized at eye level is that it is one of the better angles to shoot from. If you shoot from the bottom up, it is unflattering for most people; whereas, if you shoot from the top down, it makes you look small. It's almost always best to keep the camera straight on you.

To stabilize your camera at this angle you will need a tripod. If you purchase the twelve to eighteen-inch ring light, there should be an attachment on it that allows you to mount your phone. Recommended ring lights are also on tripods that extend from twelve inches to five or six feet, making it easy for most to set their camera at eye level whether you are sitting or standing.

After your camera is set up, you set up your audio and lighting. You will want to make sure that you've followed all of the steps laid out in the lighting chapter to make the best quality video. If you feel like your camera, your lighting, and your audio are ready, stop and take a test video before rolling. You want to be absolutely positive everything is working the way you want before going all the way through your video.

Smart Tip: Brie has an Apple Watch she can connect to her iPhone camera through the camera app. This allows her to see exactly how the shot is going to look before she starts recording. It also allows her to press the "record" button right from her spot.

Shooting a Listing

Now that you're a video celebrity, don't forget your co-stars! When it comes time to shoot a virtual tour, the focus should be the home as opposed to you. Your shots need to be set up strategically to show off the best features of the house. Feel free to have a little fun in making the home the star!

Let's say you are showing a house with an amazing kitchen, an owner's on-suite jacuzzi, and a large, finished basement. To highlight those features, you may set three specific shots that accentuate the main focuses of the house. A portion of your video will show you standing behind the kitchen counter, with the camera three feet in front of the counter. This will ensure the focus is on the counter, but you can still be seen while talking about the rest of the kitchen.

If you're willing to have some fun, you could take a video of yourself talking about the ensuite from the bathtub! This would be the one of the times that the shot could be from the top down or could be three feet in front of you showing you looking out of the tub talking to the camera. It would be a fun way to show off the jacuzzi while also talking about the rest of the ensuite, and showing a little bit of your personality.

Our suggestion for shooting a house is to choose three main points to focus on, while the rest of the shots might be you walking through the house and adding a voiceover.

Shooting While Walking

Walk throughs are a very important part of showing a house, especially at a time when ninety-five percent of Americans are currently on stay-at-home orders and cannot physically walk through a house. However, these moving shots can be extremely hard to take if you aren't sure how to take them and don't have the right equipment.

The first thing you will need is a plan. Know exactly what route you want to take through the house before you start filming. Once your plan is set, you will want to set up your gimbal. There are multiple gimbals out there that can help stabilize your shots as you are walking. These gimbals also have adapters for lights, which should take care of most of the lighting for you, but you won't really know until you start moving through the rooms.

You should start in your first room walking around slowly, and again, keeping the camera around eye level, show the entire room. If you want something to stand out a little bit more, simply walk closer to it so that it takes up more of the shot.

As mentioned earlier, most of the audio for these moving shots are going to be voiceovers. These voiceovers could be shot as you are taking the video or afterwards. If you are going to take the audio as you are walking around, you will want to mount your microphone adapter on the gimbal. You may have to purchase an extra shoe mount attachment so that you can mount both your light and your adapter securely.

To record the voiceover afterwards as recommended, you will have to do so in a separate, post-production application. You can learn more about that in the chapter on editing your video.

Shooting in the Car or Outside

You never know when a brilliant idea might strike you! You may have some exciting real estate news or you're really busy and your mind is racing through its to-do list. When the inspiration hits, it can seem to catch you at inconvenient times, either in your car or outside. But what you'll know in that moment is that you really need to get some content out. No matter the reason, if you find yourself in this situation, you will want to ensure you are still capturing quality video.

Spur of the moment videos—like a big congratulations to the family who has multiple offers above selling price—may be less "professional," and that is okay! You may be holding the phone like you are taking a selfie and that is also okay. People expect to see that type of content on their timelines. Just make sure to rely on your video best practices to be sure the quality is worthy of the audience.

If you believe you may be shooting video takes in your car on a regular basis, then it might make sense for you to buy a phone mount for your windshield. This mount will allow you to have stability of your camera, at eye level, in the car. If you know you are about to start recording a video on the phone, be sure to turn off the air conditioning or heat and, if you have it, the Bluetooth. The best part of shooting in the car is that there isn't too much background noise if you're parked, which you should be! Remember, it's illegal in most states to actively use your phone while driving, so please no videoing and driving!

Whether Rain or Shine

Outdoor shoots, as discussed in the last chapter, are a bit tough because you cannot control many of the important elements of the video, like weather and sound. Obviously, you want to try your best, but if you are walking somewhere you can't necessarily control the lighting. The sun, clouds, and wind will all act according to Mother Nature, but as long as you aren't filming in pouring rain, whipping wind, or in the middle of a marching band, people understand the occasional cloud spot or breeze. As long as you are not trying to highlight something outside, the lighting doesn't have to be perfect and neither does the audio.

Smart Tip: Use wired headphones or AirPods for walking and talking videos. There are two main reasons for this. The first is that it looks more natural. If you look at most walking and talking videos, even by large companies or celebrities, they usually wear some kind of wired headphones. The second reason is that audio from the headphones is typically good quality!

Chapter 7

Edit Your Video

Now that you have your video(s) shot, it's time to make yourself look like a star! You will learn how to take out all the "uhs, hms, and ahs" fairly easily and learn how to make your video more engaging and brand appropriate.

If you don't want to edit, that's ok too. Your videos do not need to be perfect to be effective. You can always come to this in the future.

Editing 101

There are a few reasons why you may need to edit your videos - a dog started barking, you tripped over some words, your camera shook, the lighting wasn't great, or you decided you wanted to use the video for a different platform than you originally shot for - these things happen and are common. Thankfully, with personalized pre-recorded videos, you are able to go in and make changes to your video. Some of the most common edits are:

Splitting: splits your video into two clips.

Trimming: takes some footage away from either the beginning or the end of the video

Reframing/ Resizing: allows you to change the size of the video and or change the orientation of the video

Adding Voiceovers: adding narration *after* you've shot your video

In this chapter, we will go over how to do all of these edits either on your phone or on your computer. Doing edits on your phone is the most ideal way as it allows you to edit on the go and it requires less steps. However, some people will prefer to edit on their computer because the screen is larger.

We hand-selected the platforms mentioned in this chapter based on accessibility to different devices/brands, affordability, longevity of the platform, ease of use, and functionalities. The truth, however, is that many platforms offer similar capabilities - so feel free to use the platforms that are best for YOU!

Using InShot on Your Smartphone

InShot is a rather sophisticated smartphone application that allows you to do all your post-production work right from your phone. In the app, you will see three circles at the bottom, "videos," "images," and "collage." If you select "videos," your entire video library from your phone will display for you to choose which video you want to edit. Only select the video(s) you want as part of your video.

Splitting

Once your video(s) have loaded, you will be taken to your editing screen. The first edit should cut out all of those "uhs, hms, and ahs" using the SPLIT tool. If you have a clean version of the speaking parts, it will be easier to pick and choose what to edit in the remaining video.

The SPLIT tool is located all the way to the right of your toolbar, which is right above your video timeline at the bottom of the screen. Start playing your video. When you get to a section where you messed up or that you want to cut out, simply tap "split" right before and right after that section. Then, tap the section you just split and tap "delete."

Smart Tip: It may take dragging your video timeline back and forth a few times to find the perfect places to split your video. If you accidently split at the wrong place, no worries, you can always undo the action by clicking the arrow pointing left (right above your toolbar).

Voiceovers

After you have 'split' your video to a place you are comfortable with, it's time to jump into the more fun stuff!

If you want a voiceover, tap the "music" icon and then "record." InShot gives you a countdown to tell you when to start speaking. Should you like what you record the first time, just tap the checkmark. If you don't, you just tap the "x" or the redo circle with an arrow at the end of it. If you like one part of it but not another, split the recordings like you did your earlier video by tapping the red recording square and then the split button.

Reframing Your Video

Most of the social platforms require different sizes. For example, YouTube requires a 16:9 ratio whereas Instagram requires a 1:1 ratio.

InShot can help you reframe your video to fit more than one ratio so that you can use the same video on multiple platforms. Just tap the "canvas" button then select the ratio that is best for the platform you want to use. InShot lists the recommendations for most social platforms, however a quick Google search will give you the most recent size recommendations for each one.

Adding Text

Keep your viewer engaged by adding text over your video during some of the most important points. For example, if you list five ways to get more for your house, add text that highlights each point as you are explaining it.

To add text to your video, simply tap the "text" button and the text box will appear on your video. As you start to type, the text will appear in the box. To make the text bigger, you tap the arrow on the bottom right and pull down. You can also change the angle of the text with this arrow by moving the arrow in a circular motion. It's relatively easy to change all of these settings by moving the text around with two fingers.

To change the colors, you just tap the color wheel and then the color you would like. The color ought to match your brand colors and/or have enough contrast with the background. If you want to use your brand colors but they are too close to the background color, you could add a border, shadow, or label (rectangle fill) to your text. These elements can all have custom colors as well. To use these elements, just tap the word above the colors.

It's smart to match the font of the text to your brand standards. To change the font, tap the "Aa" then scroll through the fonts until you find one you would like to use.

Be mindful of how long the text stays on top of the video. You don't want to move to the next scene and have text that doesn't reflect the updated speech. To adjust the timing, you have to adjust the green bar right above the timeline line by touching the left or right arrows.

Finishing Your Edits

Once you're done making all of your edits, you export your video by tapping the square with an arrow coming out of it in the top left corner. This will save the new, edited video to your camera roll. If you're done editing for the time being but know you will need to come back to the video later, you can hit the arrow pointing left in the top left hand corner. You will be asked if you want to Draft or Discard the video, tap "Draft."

If you are looking for a full, step-by-step tutorial, visit www.VideoEstateAgent.com to find our editing basics course.

Editing with WeVideo on Your Computer

As odd as it seems, editing gets far more complicated when you use a computer versus your phone. Computer applications and software have more functions to choose from, which can complicate your process. So before you start editing your video on your computer, just be aware that it can be very easy to get caught up in all of the options available to you.

A popular platform for video editing is WeVideo. This is a paid platform, but plans start as low as $5 per month.

When you login to WeVideo, you will be taken to your personal hub. Here you will create a new video project by selecting "video." After you make that selection, the editor will pop up. You will have your media on the left-hand side, your video on the right and your timeline on the bottom.

To get started, you will want to go to "My Media" on the left-hand side, this is where you will upload the video(s) you want to edit. Once your video uploads, you will select and drag it down onto the timeline to begin editing it.

Smart Tip: Make sure you drag it as far left as you can on the timeline so that your video starts at 0:00 and not a random time.

Splitting

Just like on your phone, you can split your video on WeVideo. But, as warned, you have many more options to choose from! To split your clip in WeVideo, you can either select and drag the blue marker to the spot where you need to split or you can play the video and use the spacebar to stop it where it needs to be split. Once you have the blue marker where it needs to be, you just select the scissors on the right-hand side of the bar to split the clip. If you need to delete a clip you've split, you select the clip and in the small toolbar that pops up above the clip, select the trash can.

Voiceovers

To add in a voiceover in WeVideo, go to your media library. Right above your videos, there is a button that says "record." After you select the record button, the record screen will show up and you can select whether or not you want to watch the video as you are recording. Once you've made your selection, you start recording by clicking the big red "record" button that replaced the video timeline on the bottom.

When you stop recording you can either delete the recording by selecting the trash can or, if you're happy with the recording, you can select the big, blue check on the right. If you select the checkmark, you will be able to split or delete the audio later on, if needed.

Reframing Your Video

To reframe your video to fit another size, select the size in the bottom right-hand side of the video viewer. The only sizes supported by WeVideo are 16:9, 9:16 and 1:1.

Adding Text

Add some eye-catching text by selecting the "A" button directly over the "record." WeVideo gives you many options for adding text to your video. Check out the left-hand side of the media screen where WeVideo has organized all of their options into four folders. From these folders, you can select "motion," "static," "in season," or "callout." For the sake of simplicity, focus on the static text.

To add static text to your video, select the static folder, select the box that says "basic text," and drag the box down to your video timeline. You will want to make sure the text box goes in the "video 2" row so it will show up over your video. Once you have the video on the timeline, you'll want to make sure it is in the right place by selecting the black box and dragging it. You can also lengthen or shorten it by hovering over the right-hand side of the video, waiting for the double-sided arrow, and dragging it to your desired length.

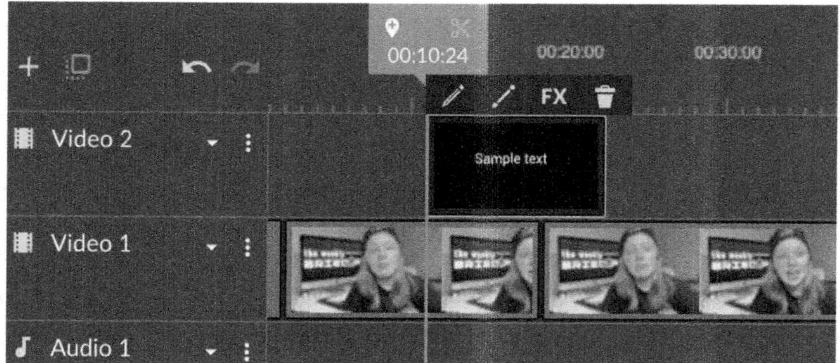

Now, to edit your text, you will need to click the pencil in the mini toolbar that shows up above the text box in the timeline. Upon selecting the pencil, the text editing box will appear where your media library once was. Type in the words you want.

Select your font by clicking the dropdown that is usually pre-set to "Roboto." Remember, make sure your font follows your brand standards as closely as possible.

Continue to showcase your brand by choosing the color of your font by selecting the "A" with a white line under it to change the font color. You could also change the text background by clicking one of the two "A" boxes next to that button and selecting the color you'd like to use.

Change the size of the text by dragging the slider on the scale next to the word "size" or type in a number next to the scale. And lastly, to change the position of the text, you just select the text on your video preview and drag it to where you want it to be.

Finishing Your Edits

When you are finished editing your video, find the blue "Finish" button in the top left corner. Upon clicking that button, the following screen will appear.

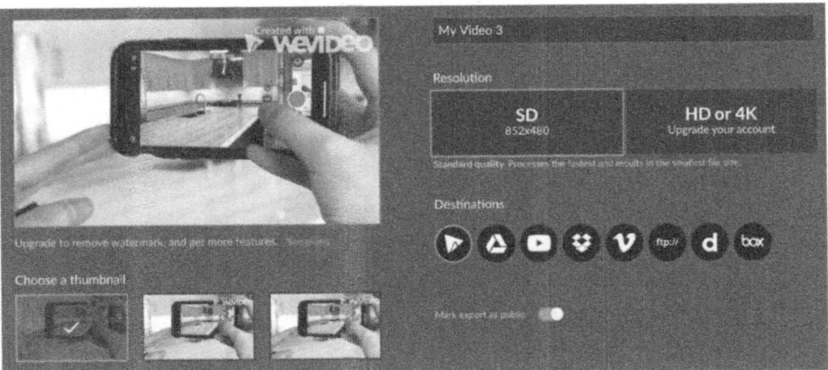

From here, select "HD or 4K" and then select "export" in the bottom left corner. If you don't do those two things, the video will live in your "exports" on WeVideo. To access the video, select "exports" from the top navigation bar. There, you select the video you want to download and in the top left corner, from the icon navigation, select the arrow pointing down. This will download the new video file straight to your computer.

Again, editing on your computer can be a bit more complicated but it also offers far more precision and functionality. If you find you prefer editing on your phone though, that is A-OK! You can still get everything done.

Chapter 8

I Made My Video, Now What?

Learn the basics of common social platforms and what content fits best.

Now that you have your video, you have to find people who will watch it. Knowing your audience is critical to choosing where, when, and how to promote your video. You may create some videos specifically for the potential home buyers you're already working with, while some of your other videos may be created with the intent to get your name (and face) in front of more people.

Before posting your video anywhere, you have to match the intent and audience of the video with that of the different platforms you have access to. Most Realtors® are going to have access to a plethora of platforms such as:

- Website
- Email list
- Facebook profile
- Facebook page
- Instagram profile
- LinkedIn profile
- YouTube channel

Each of these platforms serve different purposes and audiences, so it's important to understand each purpose so that your video fits the right platform.

Your Website

If you visit just about any Realtor® or brokerage website, the first thing you'll notice should be a photo of the Realtor®(s). Have you ever wondered why? Research shows that there is an entire part of our brain that is dedicated to recognizing faces—it's actually one of the first things humans actively seek out—within thirty minutes of being born.[1]

In a business where trust and personality can make or break your career, it's critical to get your face in front of people right away. Pictures do a great job of showing people who you are and video, when done right, can do it even better.

Consider having a video introduction on your site. This introduction can help you start building trust and confidence for your potential buyer. In fact, fifty-seven percent of consumers say they feel more confident with their purchase after watching a video. Your website has one hundred percent potential for a video introduction, and maybe even other videos!

The main thing to remember about the audience visiting your website is that they are more than likely have the intent or interest in buying a house. There will be no need to convince them to buy or sell a house, but you do need to convince them that you're the right person for the job!

See more on Using Video on Your Website in Chapter 14.

---

[1] Nottingham, Phil. "Your Business's Videos Should Include Faces. Here's Why." March 15, 2017. https://wistia.com/learn/marketing/power-of-faces-in-video.

Email Marketing

If you have an email list, congrats! You're doing something right. If not, start collecting email addresses so you can maximize your marketing options. Email lists are extremely valuable as email is one of the highest converting marketing practices to date, and emails with video have even higher conversions with about sixty-five percent of readers clicking to a site from the email.

Email lists are valuable because you've already earned some trust from the person you are emailing—enough for them to give you their email address. But not all emails are equal. Some people trust you enough to share their email address for a raffle or a potential newsletter, but they aren't necessarily as interested as people who enter their email into your Contact Me page. Segmenting your email list allows you to better serve your audience.

Because emails come from people who have different levels of trust in you, only send out content to lists that are relevant. People who contact you are likely *very* interested in buying or selling a house and could use information on mortgages and contracts or even some of the listings you have available. For the email lead from the raffle, your introduction video might be the best choice.

Your Facebook Profile

One of the places most people are comfortable posting their videos to is their Facebook profile, but it is not necessarily the best business tactic. A Facebook profile is assigned to a person, not a business. Generally, the people connected to a profile have some sort of a relationship to the person who owns the profile; they are usually friends and family. Sometimes business connections will connect on Facebook, but not always.

Make sure to evaluate why you would post your work content on Facebook. What you gain in traction may not help you gain much business. You will find this discussed in greater detail in Chapter 10.

A Facebook Page

A Facebook Page can be associated with a business or public figure, so it's important to choose which page is associated with your business. When you post your video to a Facebook Page, the video is served to people who "like" the page and people who don't already. Knowing that, you'll have to be prepared for any user on Facebook to see your video.

In the United States, about 55 percent of Facebook users are female and about twenty-three percent of them are between twenty-five to thirty-five years old, totaling between 20 and 25 million. Oddly enough, there are also about 20–25 million male users between 25–34. All of these numbers can be found using Facebook's Audience Insights tool.

According to the National Realtors® Association's 2019 study, you can assume the majority of Facebook users are nearing the age of the average first-time home buyer, which is thirty-three. Gearing your Facebook content to first-time homebuyers will help you target a wide range of this platform's users. Position yourself as an expert and share videos of some of your starter homes, not necessarily your $500,000 houses.

Instagram Profile

Unlike Facebook, Instagram Profiles are typically the same for people and businesses. However, if you choose to advertise on Instagram, it's smart to create a professional Instagram profile to use specifically for real estate.

Instagram is a fully visual platform. While captions do play a role in your performance, the majority of the content consumed is front-facing visual content, either photos or videos. Videos, however, receive about two times more engagement on average. Videos stand out because they add movement to your timeline.

Instagram is most popular among eighteen to twenty-nine-year olds and in 2019, about eighty-three percent of teens claimed Instagram to be their favorite social media platform (Hootsuite https://blog.hootsuite.com/instagram-statistics/). Does that mean you should totally discount it? Not exactly. Instagram also reaches about forty-seven percent of Americans between the ages of thirty to forty-nine. Given that the median age of *all* home buyers is forty-seven, as reported by National Realtors® Association, you shouldn't discount Instagram.

The videos posted on Instagram should be more polished and professional looking, but they can hit on many topics. Call out the architecturally pleasing listings or special features in homes you list. Other ideas could be a celebratory closing video, showing ecstatic and satisfied home buyers. Or, post an informational video featuring you sharing information on what to look for in a seller's contract.

See more on Instagram in Chapter 11.

Your LinkedIn Profile

LinkedIn is the business branded social media platform. Users are largely educated, rather well paid, and slightly older. In other words, LinkedIn is the place you should play if you are looking to sell. However, it is a tough market to break into if you're not sure what you're doing.

It's much different from all of the other channels because it's primarily a business to business platform. We can teach you how to use that to your advantage. People on LinkedIn are looking to learn and network, both of which you can help them with by using video, believe it or not. And because video is still so underutilized on LinkedIn, it performs extremely well for most people.

See more on LinkedIn in Chapter 12.

Your YouTube Channel

As the king of video, you really can't lose with your very own YouTube channel! Because YouTube is the largest video hub on the internet, it's the second largest search engine in the world. This means that most of your videos need to live on YouTube, even if you already have them on other social channels. YouTube is where you should focus your attention and build your branded video library.

YouTube allows you to create a video library fully customized by you. You create playlists for people to watch, branded graphics for your profile cover and images, and titles and descriptions for each video. All of these features allow you to convey who you are, and your expertise to your potential homebuyer.

YouTube videos turn up in the search engine results of people who have likely never heard of you. These are interested sellers and buyers looking for specific answers to their questions about real estate. You'll learn more about those questions in the chapter on YouTube.

YouTube is also one of the very best platforms for hosting large, high-quality video files. This makes it a good place to house videos you are going to share on other platforms, or to link to through email, text, or other social platforms.

See more on YouTube for Real Estate in Chapter 10.

Chapter 9

Keeping Compliant with NAR / Code of Ethics

You will learn how to stay compliant with Fair Housing laws and the Code of Ethics from the National Association of REALTORS® (NAR), which is America's largest trade association.

Why Ethics are Important in Real Estate

Trust is the foundation of relationships in real estate. Keeping compliant with a strong code of ethics, whether from a professional association like NAR, or a broader umbrella like the code of conduct from the Better Business Bureau, shows you can be trusted. Codified ethics also help guide your actions, especially when you are unsure, or simply unknowledgeable, about potential issues.

This ethical standard should extend to your online presence. If you think what you post online is only for your friends and family, think again. Videos, photographs, and even comments posted online are never really private. They are also never really personal either. What you say online may represent you in your personal life, but it can follow you into your professional life. To ensure the safety and comfort of clients/potential clients, colleagues, competitors, and communities, it is vital that you always treat everyone ethically and fairly. This will help maintain a level of professionalism, and a standard of behavior, that people can trust. Again, real estate is an industry built on trust.

As a real estate agent and/or Realtor®, you have an ethical obligation to put your clients' needs first and to promote your clients' interests at all times. *You* are your reputation in this business. Maintaining a high level of ethical standards will protect your reputation, but it will also protect everyone else. According to the National Association of Realtors® (NAR),[2] the best rule of thumb is the Golden Rule: Do unto others as you would have done to you. Treat others the way you want to be treated. Be fair, be honest, be kind. This shouldn't stop as soon as you get online.

Wherever there is a lot of money, there are always a few people willing to skirt the rules. But far more common is when real estate agents unknowingly break the rules. If you are like most agents, you are just learning how to post professionally online, so it's understandable if you unintentionally make mistakes. Plus, there's a learning curve to following NAR policies on social media. For example, one of the biggest mistakes is when an agent does not identify their brokerage. Even though this seems minor, if you break rules it could cost you big money! It could also cost you your reputation. As a Realtor®, you could lose your certifications and designations.

[2] "2020 Code of Ethics & Standards of Practice." National Association of Realtors®®, January 1, 2020. https://www.nar.Realtor®/about-nar/governing-documents/code-of-ethics/2020-code-of-ethics-standards-of-practice.

Common Mistakes

There is a difference between business casual and friend casual, even online. The following are common mistakes made in social media posts that can get you into trouble:

- Venting about clients, commissions, competitors, or your community. It is best to leave the negative alone. Focus on the positive, no matter how tempting it might be to complain. This should apply to your posts and your comments on what others post.
- Never post private information—yours or someone else's—ever.
- Sharing another agent's listing without their permission. This can happen even unintentionally. For example, posting about going to an open house that isn't your open house is not permitted. It is best to get the listing agent's permission before posting anything, period.
- Be mindful of what you post on your personal accounts. According to the NAR,[3] "if you're in doubt, include a link in the post to a webpage that displays your company's logo prominently." This keeps you in compliance with the standards and codes of ethics.
- Follow all state/federal/organizational standards when it comes to posting listings that are "coming soon."

---

[3] Kellogg, Melissa M. "Social Media Posts That Get You in Trouble," Realtor® Magazine (The National Association of Realtors®®, March 7, 2016), https://magazine.Realtor®/law-and-ethics/feature/article/2016/03/social-media-posts-that-get-you-in-trouble.

NAR Policies

Here's an overview of ethics codes as they relate to suggested NAR video policies:[4]

- Social media posts (even informal discussions in comments) are treated as marketing under the NAR Code of Ethics and Standards of Practice. Maintain the same level of ethical codes and standards of practice as you do offline. For example, never post anything confidential or private involving financial information, or any other information given in confidence or protected by privacy laws.
- Your professional affiliation should be clearly noted in every post, video, and comments you make on others' posts. For the NAR Code of Ethics and Standards, this can be as simple as a link back to a clear logo with your professional information.
- However, for the Real Estate License Act, the "one click away" rule does not apply. Your full name, contact information, and business affiliation should be in every video. Check your license law for further requirements.[5] It is important that you always list your affiliation, accreditations, licenses, and designations honestly and accurately.
- If you are part of a franchise company, you must display the full name of the brokerage, not just the franchise's name.

---

[4] "Create a Social Media Usage Policy," www.nar.Realtor® (The National Association of Realtors®®, n.d.), https://www.nar.Realtor®/ae/manage-your-association/association-policy/create-a-social-media-usage-policy.

[5] Aydt, Bruce. "6 Top Ethics Issues Today," Realtor® Magazine (The National Association of Realtors®®, July 13, 2016), https://magazine.Realtor®/law-and-ethics/ethics/article/2016/07/6-top-ethics-issues-today.

- Your email signature should always show all required affiliations according to NAR specifications. They may include many of the following:[6]
    - Name and/or logo of brokerage
    - Name of broker
    - Address of the brokerage office with which you, the agent, are affiliated
    - Phone/fax/email of the brokerage office. (Check how your email signature looks from your phone as well as from your computer. Sometimes, an email sent from a mobile phone will not show the same signature as the same email sent from your computer).
    - Name of the agent responsible for the website
    - State of licensure
    - Agents affiliated with a team (you may also include the name of that team)
    - Phone/fax/email of agent or team responsible for the website
    - Any other requirements mandated by state law/regulation
    - Any additional brokerage identification requirements
- The Code of Ethics and Standard of Practice 6-1 requires disclosure of any financial benefit you receive for referring someone for a service if you refer them in a media post, comment, and/or video.
- When in doubt, disclose. As a Realtor®, you should disclose things you recognize that aren't within the scope of your license when

---

[6] "Create a Social Media Usage Policy," www.nar.Realtor®realtor (The National Association of Realtor®Realtors®, n.d.), https://www.nar.Realtor®realtor/ae/manage-your-association/association-policy/create-a-social-media-usage-policy.

listing a property online. For example, if your client has a question about a home's foundation issues, refer the client to a structural engineer.[7]

- Anything you post may be reposted without your permission and may be used for purposes you never intended. Be aware of this before posting anything. This is where keeping a strict adherence to all ethical standards can keep you from getting into trouble.
- Follow all regulations per site, as well as per local, state, federal, and organizational guidelines when using social media for business purposes. Your broker and local organization should be able to guide you if you are unsure.
- Make your own content or you could be guilty of violating copyright laws. Do not use graphics, photos, or video content without written permission from the original source. If you alter a graphic, get permission to do so.

---

[7] Aydt, "6 Top Ethics Issues Today," Realtor® Magazine.

Fair Housing Act

"The Fair Housing Act declares a national policy of fair housing throughout the United States. The law makes illegal any discrimination in the sale, lease or rental of housing, or making housing otherwise unavailable, because of race, color, religion, sex, handicap, familial status, or national origin."[8]

As Realtors®, it is our duty to provide equal, professional services for all people.

Article 10 of the National Association of Realtors® Code of Ethics[9] provides that, "Realtors® shall not deny equal professional services to any person for reasons of race, color, religion, sex, handicap, familial status, national origin, sexual orientation, or gender identity. Realtors® shall not be parties to any plan or agreement to discriminate against a person or persons on the basis of race, color, religion, sex, handicap, familial status, national origin, sexual orientation, or gender identity. Realtors®, in their real estate employment practices, shall not discriminate against any person or persons on the basis of race, color, religion, sex, handicap, familial status, national origin, sexual orientation, or gender identity."

---

[8] "What Everyone Should Know About Equal Opportunity Housing," www.nar.Realtor® (The National Association of Realtors®®, n.d.), https://www.nar.Realtor®/fair-housing/fair-housing-program/what-everyone-should-know-about-equal-opportunity-housing.

[9] "2020 Code of Ethics & Standards of Practice." National Association of Realtors®, January 1, 2020. https://www.nar.Realtor®/about-nar/governing-documents/code-of-ethics/2020-code-of-ethics-standards-of-practice.

When you are planning and shooting your videos, make sure you are also staying within your state and federal guidelines of The Fair Housing Act.

The best and easiest way to do this is to never say anything on video that you wouldn't say at a showing or in front of an authority figure. The only thing worse than saying it is having it recorded and broadcast to the world!

Chapter 10

YouTube for Realtors®

Learn how to use the second most powerful search engine in the world and why it also acts as your video library.

YouTube is the second largest search engine in the world. If your clients aren't searching Google, they are certainly searching YouTube. Google owns YouTube, so Google is okay with the "competition" because they still make money from the views. It's not surprising that as you search Google, YouTube videos will show up in the search results! According to Searchmetrics, YouTube's visibility in search results is more than double what it was two years ago.

If you do it correctly, YouTube can drive some serious traffic to your website (that you don't have to pay for.) And we know that the more people who go to your website, the more potential home buyers you will capture!

Setting Up Your Channel

If you don't have your YouTube channel set up yet, fear not, you are about to learn how. The first step is setting up a Gmail account that you are okay having connected to your real estate business. Once your Gmail account is set up, go to YouTube on your computer, and in the top right-hand corner click 'Sign Up.'

When prompted, you should sign in with your real estate-focused Gmail account. Now your YouTube account is created! To create your channel, select your icon in the top right corner. A dropdown menu will appear, from here you will select "Your Channel."

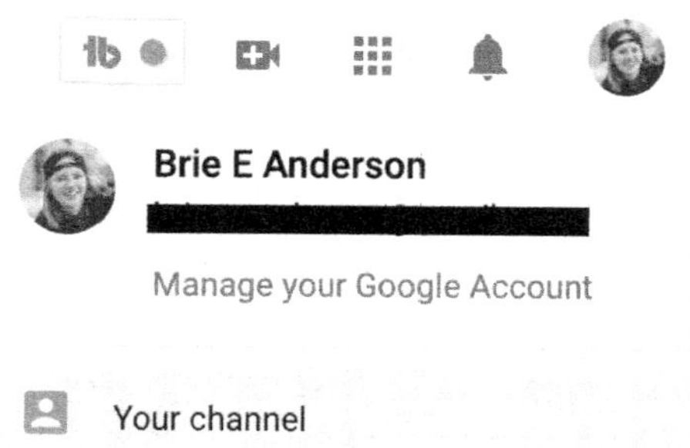

After creating your YouTube channel, you will want to customize it to match your brand. Your channel name should be the name you give out to your clients. That way the channel pops up when they Google you.

The next thing to change is your channel photo, which should be your headshot. The best size for this photo is 800 x 800 px. The other photo is your channel art. This is the 2560 x 1440 px banner across the top of your channel. This is the optimal size, but it shrinks down to the middle 1546 x 423 px. Using a platform like Canva to create banner art is easy because they provide premade templates you can customize to your liking. Don't worry, that's all the art you will need!

Smart Tip: If you are not prompted to create a banner, go to your channel and select the blue "customize channel" button.

Description and Links

You will want to write a description of 100-400 words for your About section. This will act as your introduction to people who've not met you before, so you will want to provide a quick overview of who you are (in plain English). Avoid jargon and try to share a little bit about what you value. In this section, you will also want to be sure to list the type of services you offer and the kind of work you do. Once your About is to your liking, add in links to your website and your social media platforms.

YouTube Introduction Video

The first video you should post to your YouTube channel is your introduction video. This video should be a quick 30-60 second video explaining who you are and what you do. Access YouTube from your computer and click the video camera with a plus sign inside of it. Select 'upload a video' (not livestream). You can either drag the video file onto the screen or click the 'select files' button to choose the file from your computer's file list.

Uploading Your Video

When you upload your video, you will be shown a screen that allows you to describe your video in multiple ways to both people and Google. The screen looks like this:

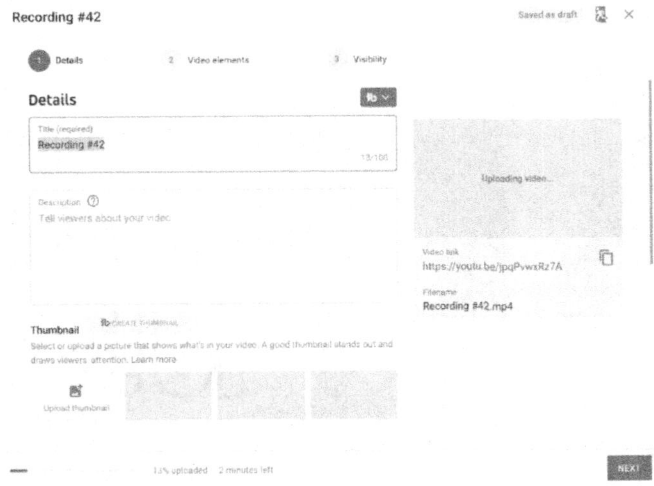

Your title for your introduction video will be different from most of your videos as the introduction video is mainly used for your channel, not for search. This title should be welcoming your channel guests. A simple "Welcome to Sold by Jane Doe Real Estate" will work just fine.

Smart Tip: Your title can be changed at any time, so you're not stuck with it forever. But it's not recommended to change it frequently.

In the 'Description' box, give a brief description about you in about 200 words or less. The description of your video shows up right underneath the video player when a viewer is watching your video.

Upload a **thumbnail**, a 1280 x 720 graphic, that is shown in the search results. It should explain your video with a picture and three to four words (ideally).

In this example, the thumbnail shows the real estate agent with a graphic of a key and a contract. Just from the pictures alone, you could likely guess what the video is about. Then the oversized words "home buying" tell you exactly what you're going to learning the video.

An even better thumbnail would have a bigger face that is more in focus, a few less words and one specific word that stands out.

Your introduction video thumbnail may be a photo of you where your face is very visible, and your name. You want the text to be easy to read, so always add an outline or a background behind it. One of our favorite places to make these thumbnails is on Canva. See the example we created in Canva below.

If you scroll past the thumbnail, you'll see the option to add your video to a playlist. You can skip that section for this video. After that section is the Audience section where it is extremely important to mark that your videos are not made for children. This keeps you compliant with a recent act called Children Online Privacy Protection Act (COPPA). It ensures your video won't be mixed into childrens' playlists.

Now, select 'next' in the bottom right-hand side twice. This will allow you to skip section '2.' In section '3,' select 'Save or Publish,' select 'Public,' then 'Publish'. Now your video can be viewed by your future clients!

Make sure to pin your introduction video on your channel. Click on your profile picture in the top right-hand corner and select 'Your Channel' from the dropdown. Select 'Customize Channel' located under your channel art. Your channel will become editable and a blue box will appear that says, 'Feature Content'. Select that box and then select your introduction video. Now your introduction video, along with its title and description, will be the first thing customers see.

What to Post Next (and Next, and Next)

Determining what kind of content to create and publish is really tough sometimes. With YouTube, there are a plethora of tools you can use to find topics for your videos.

Google Trends

The first tool we are going to talk about is Google Trends. As we stated earlier in the book, YouTube is the second largest search engine. It's also owned by Google. The data Google provides about search trends can be really helpful.

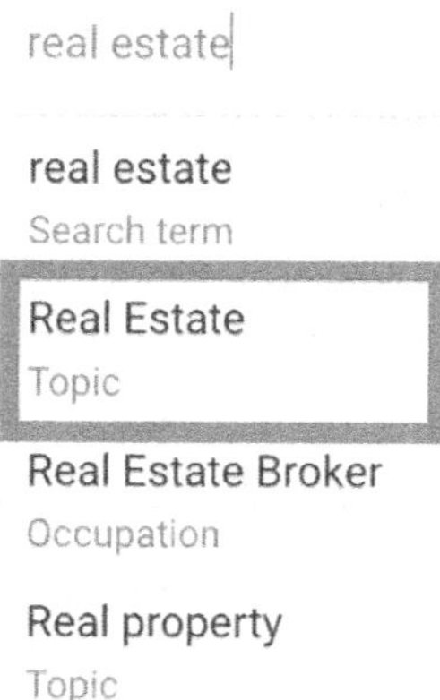

To get to Google Trends, just go to www.trends.google.com. When you get there, in the box that says, 'Enter a search term or a topic' type 'real estate.' A dropdown will auto-generate, make sure you select the box that says, 'Real Estate Topic.'

After selecting 'Real Estate Topic,' a chart will show up. Above the chart there will be four options that say, 'United States,' 'Past 12 months,' 'All categories,' and 'Web Search.'

We are going to customize these options. First, select 'United States.' A box will open up that will allow you to type in a city you service. Next, select 'Web search' and from the dropdown select 'YouTube search.'

Smart Tip: Depending on the city/location you select, these changes may narrow the audience too much and limit the amount of information that gets generated. If this happens, change the location to the next largest location (city to county to state).

Once you're set up and getting information, you will need to scroll to the bottom of the page and find 'Related topics' and 'Related queries.' Looking through these, you will want to take note of any of the topics you think you may be able to speak on as these are the hottest search topics at the moment in your area.

TubeBuddy

After gathering a baseline of ideas, TubeBuddy is a great tool for narrowing down the topics you can (and should) create videos about. TubeBuddy is an online platform and extension that provides insights for YouTube channel owners on keywords and best practices. (Extensions are small software programs that customize the browsing experience.) Keywords are the words that people use to attempt to find content—they are very important and will be referred to often throughout the rest of this chapter. To get the TubeBuddy extension, you will go to: chrome.google.com/webstore and search TubeBuddy in the top left corner. Once you find the extension, simply click 'Add to Chrome.' Your Chrome browser will now have a small TubeBuddy icon to the right of the search bar. These are your extensions.

The next time you go to YouTube, to the left of your profile picture in the top right corner, you will see a gray icon with a "tb" in it. This is where you will login to TubeBuddy, or you will be directed to TubeBuddy to create an account.

Now that you're set up, you'll be able to get started on your keyword research. To get started, take one of the topics you found in Google Trends, or an idea that you already have, and search it on YouTube. TubeBuddy will automatically add statistics to the right-hand column of the search result page after you click the blue 'Show Keyword Score' button. The stats will show, at a glance, the search volume and competition. Search volume is how often the keyword is searched and competition shows the chances of that particular word or phrase showing up in searches. Under those two scales there is an "overall" scale that weighs the possibility of hitting the top of the search results. The higher you rank in the search results, the more people have a chance to view your video.

Smart Tip: It should be noted that TubeBuddy does limit the number of searches you can do per day - for unlimited searches, you can upgrade to one of TubeBuddy's three paid plans.

The hope is that you will find a topic with a score over 50. It's likely that this will take a bit of time to find. In this example, we searched "real estate investment." The overall score is 13; not too great. There are a ton of searches, but also a lot of competition. Thankfully, TubeBuddy also lays out related searches for you to try to find an opportunity keyword. So we selected "real estate investing for beginners." We get a bit closer with this keyword as we hit 25, and one level deeper "real estate investing for beginners 2020" got a 58!

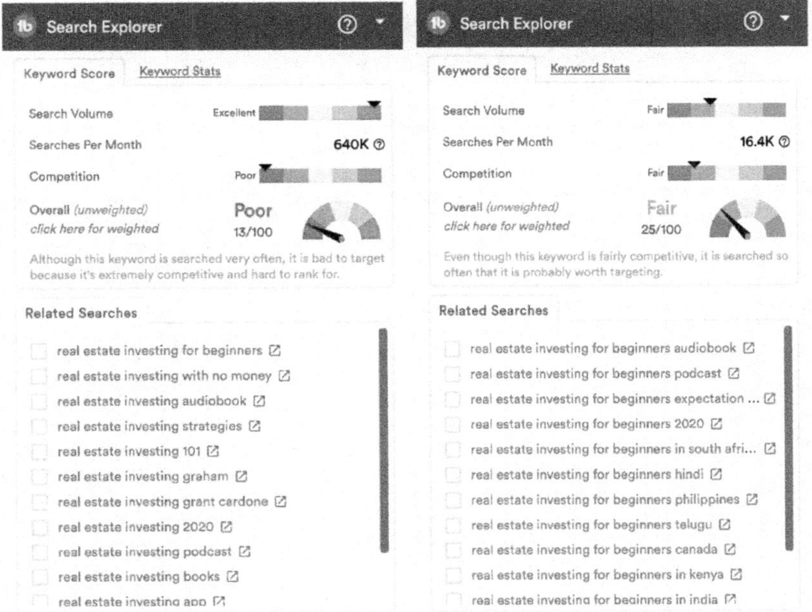
Search Explorer
Keyword Score
Keyword Stats
Search Volume
Excellent
Searches Per Month
640K
Competition
Poor
Overall (unweighted)
click here for weighted
Poor
13/100
Although this keyword is searched very often, it is bad to target because it's extremely competitive and hard to rank for.
Related Searches
real estate investing for beginners
real estate investing with no money
real estate investing audiobook
real estate investing strategies
real estate investing 101
real estate investing graham
real estate investing grant cardone
real estate investing 2020
real estate investing podcast
real estate investing books
real estate investing app
Search Explorer
Keyword Score
Keyword Stats
Search Volume
Fair
Searches Per Month
16.4K
Competition
Fair
Overall (unweighted)
click here for weighted
Fair
25/100
Even though this keyword is fairly competitive, it is searched so often that it is probably worth targeting.
Related Searches
real estate investing for beginners audiobook
real estate investing for beginners podcast
real estate investing for beginners expectation ...
real estate investing for beginners 2020
real estate investing for beginners in south afri...
real estate investing for beginners hindi
real estate investing for beginners philippines
real estate investing for beginners telugu
real estate investing for beginners canada
real estate investing for beginners in kenya
real estate investing for beginners in india

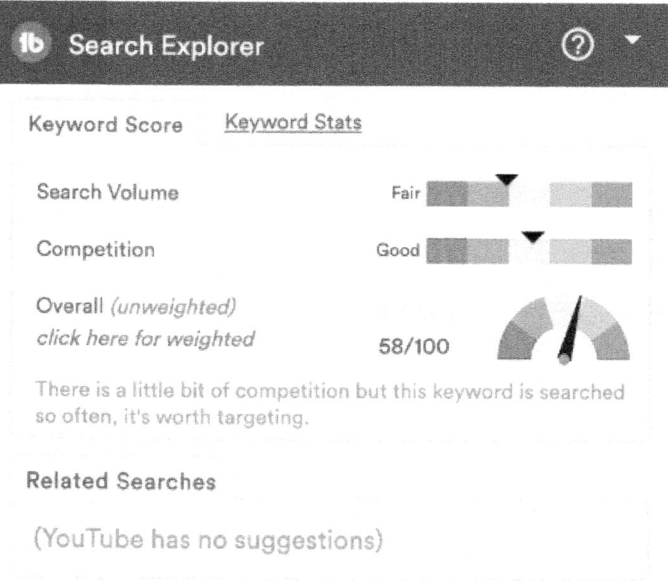

So, get to creating! You've got the perfect topic.

The Upload Checklist

After you've created the video for your opportunity keyword, it's time to upload your video. Posting this video is going to be much different than posting your introduction video.

Titling Best Practices

Use the opportunity keyword you just discovered on TubeBuddy in your title, and use it as close to the beginning as possible. This is critical because it tells YouTube your video is one hundred percent about that word or phrase.

It's not just YouTube's attention you have to capture, you also have to grab the attention of people searching on YouTube. Some tricks for capturing searchers' attention is:

- Put one word in all caps
- Use numbers when applicable
- Use parentheses when possible

Ex: Real Estate Investing for Beginners in 2020 (3 EASY STEPS)

Ex: Real Estate Investing for BEGINNERS in 2020 (& beyond)

Our eyes are trained to find things that don't belong. When we are looking at/for words and letters, our eyes are immediately drawn to the symbols and numbers.

Description Best Practices

Descriptions should be somewhere between 200-400 words. The first two sentences are the most important though, as those are the two that viewers see before the "read more..." prompt. A lot of the time, people will put a call to action in those first two lines, either a link to another YouTube video or to a page on their website where people can opt into something (like a downloadable form, etc).

The rest of your description should include a description of your video, including a timestamp breakdown of what you cover in your video. Lastly, make sure you always have a "let's connect" section where you drop links to all of the places people can connect with you.

Thumbnail Best Practices

Your thumbnail should be 1280 x 720 and it should include the following:

- A picture of your face should be on the left
- Three or four words that are easy to read on the right

- A focus color that you use for all of your videos around those topics (more on this later)
- Use high contrast colors to make your words pop
- *Remember the rule of thirds*

The rule of thirds states that your objects should be centered in the middle of one of the nine rectangles created by both the horizontal and vertical thirds. The other option is to place the objects centered on one of the intersections.

One of the best places to create these thumbnails is Canva. When you pop into Canva, you will be asked what you are creating - select YouTube Thumbnail. From the editing screen you can add text, photos, or even a premade template, making it the perfect place to get started.

Creating Playlists

A playlist is a group of videos that all hit on a similar topic. For instance, you may have a playlist called "Tips for First Time Home Buyers," a playlist for "Home Financing Tips," or a list for "DIY Home Value Projects." Create those playlists with keywords in mind.

Ideally, every video you create should go into a playlist. People will find a video that belongs to a playlist and will find it so interesting that they may binge watch your videos. The increase in view time will not only help you build trust with YouTube and encourage YouTube to show your videos more often, but it will also help you build trust with the viewer! Specifically, the viewer who could be a potential home buyer.

More options

Click the blue "more options" prompts to find important functions.

Tags

Tags tell YouTube what your video is about. YouTube can't watch videos as they are uploaded, so they rely on the information the uploader gives them. If you have TubeBuddy Pro, TubeBuddy will generate tag ideas for you, these tags are a good place to start. The best place to gather tags, though, is the YouTube result pages.

The same way you looked for your opportunity keyword, you will find the tags you should use. Search the keyword you want and TubeBuddy will show you the most popular tags for that keyword. Make sure you use at least the top three. After those three, you should have the title of your video as a tag, a few keywords that describe your video, then your name and your channel name or playlist name.

Section 2

After you fill out your tags, you will select the "next" button in the bottom right-hand corner.

End Screen

The next section shows you two options, the first one is an end screen. End screens allow you to urge viewers to subscribe to your channel and/or view another video of yours. To add your end screen elements, select "add" at the end of the row.

YouTube automatically cuts out the last twenty seconds of your video as this is the only time you can show end screen elements. To add your end screen element, select the plus sign next in the bottom left

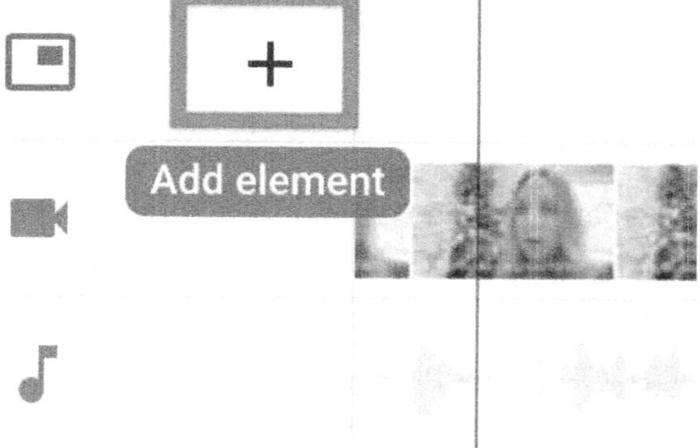

corner.

You will be given options of what kind of elements to add—video, playlist, subscribe, or channel.

You should always use subscribe, and either video or playlist. We want people to keep up to date and engaged with your video, so both of these options are helpful! Whether you choose a specific video, the best video for the user, the most recent video, or a specific playlist doesn't matter too much. It is best practice, however, to try to suggest something that is relevant to the video you just showed the viewer.

Cards

The next option in Section 2 is to "Add Cards." Cards can be used to promote videos or playlists, to promote other channels, or to host a poll. You want to make sure all of your videos have information cards because they act as a call-to-action to your viewer. You select a relevant time in your video for a small callout to come across the top right corner; the text in the callout should be prompting the user to do something.

To add cards to your video, in section 2, in the "Add Cards" row, select "add." On this new screen, you will be able to watch your video and select the best place to have your card show up, or if you already know where you want the card to show up, you can simply select the gray bar on the video timeline and drag it to the place you want it to be. Once you've selected your time mark for the card to enter, you have to select "Add Card" to the right of your video preview. You will then be prompted to select a video, playlist, channel, or poll to send people to.

It's best to only use videos or playlists. After selecting "video or playlist," a list of all of your videos and playlists will show up for you to select from. You will also be able to customize the card text at the bottom of this splash screen by selecting "Customize the teaser text and/or add a custom message." Two lines will pop up and you will want to type in the one that says "Teaser Text" above it—a short call to action (like the one seen in the photo above) will work. To finalize this card, select "create card" in the bottom right hand corner. Then, to get back to the publishing screen, select "Return to YouTube Studio" next to your profile photo in the top right-hand corner.

Now we're ready to move on to Section 3! Just select "next" from the Section 2 screen and you will be taken to your publishing options (Section 3).

Posting Strategies

So, you have your video and now it is ready to be sent out into the world! But before you send it, you want to make sure you have a plan for getting it in front of people. YouTube is pretty tough on creators and if your video doesn't do very well in the first twenty-four hours and then again over the next seven days, YouTube will push your video to the back burner. With that in mind, you want to make sure you have a plan.

Post When People Will Watch

If you're like us, the entire upload process may take longer than expected the first few times. And if you started the process at eight p.m. and the video isn't ready until ten p.m., you have to ask yourself whether or not people are going to be willing to watch it (all the way through) at ten o'clock at night. If the answer is no, then you would be better off scheduling the video to go live at a later time.

The best viewing time for most people is first thing in the morning around seven or eight a.m., around lunch from eleven a.m. to noon or right between dinner and bedtime, roughly six or seven p.m. Scheduling your video also allows you to plan how you are going to promote after it goes live.

Have a Schedule

One way to ensure people will watch your video when it comes out is to have a consistent posting schedule. In YouTube's perfect world, every creator would post at least once a week at the same time every week.

For instance, Brie posts a video every Sunday at seven p.m. Her audience knows that if they tune in after seven on Sunday there will be new content for them to watch. YouTube knows that this video will be coming out, so they will have something to push at that time to her audience. Many successful YouTube creators will have their posting schedule listed on their Channel Art and listed in the description on all of their videos. You can even give your posting schedule on the end screen of your videos.

So, pick a time when you will be able to post every single week and remember, in section 3, you can always schedule your video to go out later by selecting "Schedule" instead of "Save or Publish." YouTube will give you a calendar that makes choosing your date and time super easy. Once you have your date and time selected, just click "Schedule" in the bottom left corner to get your video scheduled.

Create Series

The best way to keep a consistent schedule that keeps people engaged is to create content that they are going to expect. If you post the suggested one video a week, you may have one or two "series" you focus on. For example, you could talk about subjects for buyers on the first and third Friday of every week and subjects for sellers on the second and fourth Friday.

One way to come up with a series is to plan what playlists you'd like to have before you even create videos. Using the TubeBuddy tool, you could find ten to twenty video topics. From those, group them into potential series for your YouTube Channel. Those will be your playlists and, in turn, the series you will work to create over the next several weeks.

Now you have a publishing schedule you can share with your audience so that they have something to look forward to.

Cross-Posting

As we mentioned earlier, YouTube is a great place for hosting your long-form videos. However, the majority of your views for these videos are going to come from you promoting the videos through other channels.

As soon as your video goes live, you will want to share it on your Facebook profile, Facebook page and LinkedIn profile. Remember, each of these serve a different purpose. Your Facebook profile will likely get you fast and high engagement as your friends and family will engage because they know and like you. Your Facebook page will get you a few views as well, but most of those views will come in a few hours to a few days, not right away. LinkedIn will be hit or miss, but if your caption is good, it can really reach a lot of people and rack up some views. We will go over each of these platforms in depth in the coming chapters.

Consider if the videos serve a purpose on your website. Sometimes the videos you create may be a good fit for your Frequently Asked Questions page, your introduction page, a listing page or a process page.

If it doesn't fit in any of those places, ask yourself if it could create a good blog post to live on your website. Check out this highly recommended tactic in chapter, 14 Videos on Your Website.

Chapter 11

Facebook Video for Real Estate

Find out how to use Facebook as a strategy and as a useful tool for video.

Facebook is extremely popular, with about eight million video views per day.[10] Nearly eighty-five percent of those views will be done 'on silent'—the viewer will not hear any of the content. Square-shaped videos encourage views about thirty-five percent more than landscape views, according to Buffer.[11] Live video, on average, gets about four times the views than pre-recorded videos (Facebook.) And overall, Facebook favors videos in their algorithm, likely because video encourages engagement. If you are creating video, Facebook is a no-brainer.

We've talked about the difference between Facebook Pages and Facebook Profiles in previous chapters, and chances are most businesspeople will have one, if not both, of these profiles, which is highly recommended for real estate professionals. Facebook has guides for both in their Help Center.

Your YouTube Videos on Facebook

The videos you create for your YouTube Channel will play a major role in the content you post on Facebook. Instead of creating all new content

---

[10] Aslam, Salman. "Facebook by the Numbers: Stats, Demographics & Fun Facts." (OmniCore Agency, April 22,2020). https://www.omnicoreagency.com/facebook-statistics/.

[11] Peters, Brian. "Does Vertical Video Make a Difference? We Spent $6,000 on Tests to Find Out Does Vertical Video Make a Difference? We Spent $6,000 on Tests to Find Out." Resources. April 02, 2019. https://buffer.com/resources/vertical-video.

for Facebook videos, we'll teach you how to make your YouTube videos work for Facebook.

The easiest way to share your YouTube video to your Facebook Page is to copy the YouTube link and paste it into a post on your Facebook Page. Facebook will automatically bring up the thumbnail of the video and the title. As soon as those features are generated, you can delete the link from your post and the video will still be there.

YOUTUBE.COM

How to Keep Your Business ALIVE in 2020 (Digital Marketing Strategies)

Ideally, you'll want to post to your Facebook Page within an hour of posting your video to YouTube so that you can start getting views right away. As soon as you post it to your Facebook Page, share that post to your Facebook Profile. This signals to Facebook the post is engaging (because the post has been shared) and because your friends and family are the most likely to engage with your content. Every like, comment, etc. on the post you share to your profile will reflect very well on your Page's post.

Square Videos

One way to promote your YouTube video is by splitting it into a short thirty-second preview and creating a square video using the preview. The preview may be just a clip of an interesting point you made or even just your video introduction. Gary Vee has some great examples of square videos. You may want to check some out.

You're going to want to create a square video with a catchy title on the top, your landscape preview video in the middle and open (as in always showing) captions on the bottom. You can make these videos by going to Canva.com and selecting "Instagram Post" and then "Blank Template."

First, we'll need to upload your video to Canva. On the edit screen, drag and drop your preview file onto the screen to upload it, or select "Uploads" from the menu on the left. A button will populate at the top of the menu that says "upload your image or video" that allows you to select the file from your computer to upload.

After uploading your video, make it big enough to be the width of the screen by clicking the video, selecting one of the small circles that shows up on the corner, and dragging down. Once it's big enough, select the video and drag it towards the middle of the graphic. When the two guidelines appear and intersect, the video is centered and where it should be. Alternately, you can click "position," and then click "middle" and your video will be centered on the page.

Now, add your title by selecting "text" from the menu on the left-hand side. The title just needs to be something that catches people's attention - it could be a quote, a quick description of what you're talking about, etc.

The words on the bottom (the captions) cannot be added in Canva, so use a tool like Quicc or Zubtitle to add those in later. Once you have your video and title the way you like them, you are ready to download your new video file by selecting "Download" in the top right corner.

The file you download from Canva will be the one you upload to either Quicc or Zubtitle, which are online automatic video captioning services, to get captioned. Once you have your captions on your video, you will be ready to post to your Facebook Page!

When you post your square video to Facebook, write a short caption that ends with something similar to "see the first comment for the full video" and post it *without* your YouTube link. Then, right after you post your video, you will comment the YouTube link in the first comment. Facebook does not like when people try to suggest people leave Facebook by posting links in their posts, so they tend to hide those posts a little more. The link in the comment, however, is not seen as part of the post, and therefore doesn't hurt your chances of showing up as much.

Again, once you post to your business Facebook page, you will want to then share it to your personal Facebook profile to get some initial engagement right away.

Posting Videos to Facebook

After about two weeks, you will be set to upload your full YouTube video FILE (not the link, the actual file) to your Facebook page as the YouTube hype for your current audience will have likely died down. If you don't have a YouTube channel and you are just creating videos to post to Facebook, but you have a video ready, this is the information you've been waiting for.

Just like YouTube, it's important to post your video by going to your Facebook Page on your computer and clicking into the box that says, "Write a Post." When you click into that box, on the bottom right-hand side, select "Photo/Video," and then select the video you want to upload from your computer.

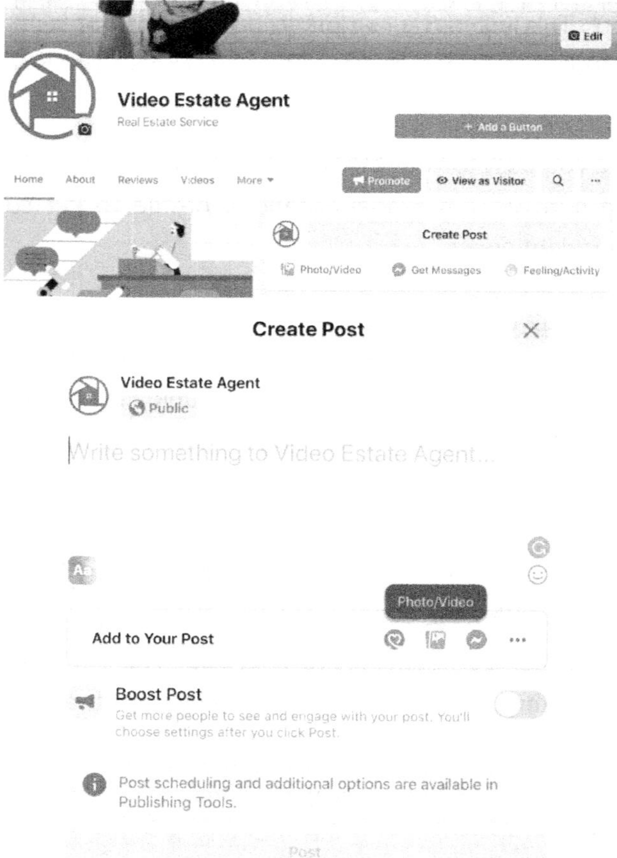

After selecting the video and selecting "open" you will be shown a video upload screen that looks somewhat similar to the one YouTube uses. Add a title to the video that is optimized for engaging people who scroll past it—the same rules used for YouTube apply to this title. Use a word in all caps, and use numbers and parentheses if applicable. The *description* for this video will be much different from YouTube videos, however, as the description on Facebook is the post that goes with the video in the timeline. The wording should catch viewers' attention by asking a question, using an emoji or having some sort of shock factor that leaves people wanting more (think "I can't believe I didn't know this!").

Tags

The last section shown on this page is for *tags*. Tags are how Facebook organizes their content, so you want to be sure to use two or three relevant tags, one of them will likely be "real estate & real estate listings." When you start to type in this box, Facebook provides you with the tags that use those letters or words. Be sure to select from those tags and not try to create your own.

Thumbnails

Now select "thumbnail" from the right-hand menu. You can choose from one of the auto-generated video captures, upload your own thumbnail, or hand select a video frame to use as your thumbnail. You will see three choices: "Auto-Generated Image," "Custom Image," and "Video Frame." "Auto-generated image" allows you to simply choose from several auto-generated images, "custom image" allows you to upload your own image to use as a thumbnail, and "video frame" will bring up your video and allow you to choose a particular frame. We suggest using your own "Custom Image" thumbnails, as you will get more views. This is because custom thumbnails grab the attention of people scrolling through their timeline.

Under the thumbnail portion of the menu is "subtitles & captions." When you get to this screen, select your language, select "auto-generate" and then check the box under it that says "Auto-generate captions for future uploads." This will ensure that every video you upload will be captioned. This is important because, as we stated earlier, about eight-five percent of views happen with the sound *off*. However, if you don't have any words playing in one of your videos, obviously there is no reason to worry about captions.

All of the other options in the right-hand navigation are optional and a bit more complicated. Use these when you are comfortable with what you're already doing and are ready to explore more advanced options. Instead of working down the rest of that navigation bar, it's time to go to "2. Publishing Options" in the top navigation.

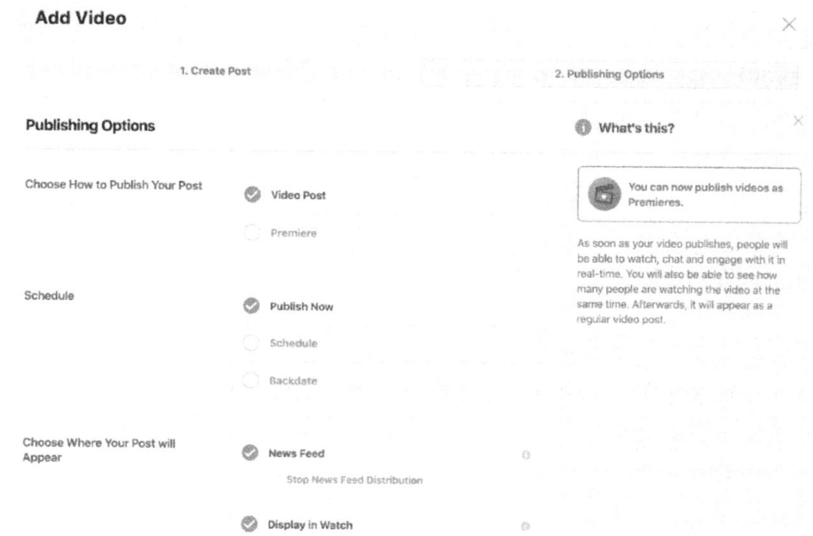

From this screen, choose whether you want to schedule your video or push it out right away. Remember, post when people are online. On Facebook, the Premiere option (above scheduling) is also a good feature as it allows people to interact with the video as if it were "live."

With the exception of the "playlists" section, use the pre-filled options in this section. For "playlists," set them up on Facebook for the same reason you would on YouTube—you want people to binge your videos! The more people watch your videos, the more they will trust you and playlists are a perfect way to keep viewers engaged. Make sure you keep all of the content in playlists relevant to one another.

Suggested real estate playlists for Facebook:

- Client testimonials
- Listing tours
- Q&A for buyers
- Q&A for sellers
- Meet my team

If you want to see great examples of Facebook videos, specifically Facebook video playlists, check out Leigh Brown's Facebook Page. She has done an amazing job of curating videos for her clients and her peers.

After all of the options are set up the way you want them, schedule using the button in the bottom right that says "schedule." Then, as always, right after your video goes live on your Facebook Page, share it to your Facebook Profile for instant engagement.

Facebook Live

This is the gem of Facebook. Your pre-recorded videos will reach *some* people, but live video is a completely different ball game. Since the COVID-19 pandemic, some countries have seen Facebook Live viewership almost double (Facebook). And whether or not people tune in to watch your video live, the video still lives on your Facebook page (if you want it to) after you finish the live session. Then you can promote that video the same way you promote other videos.

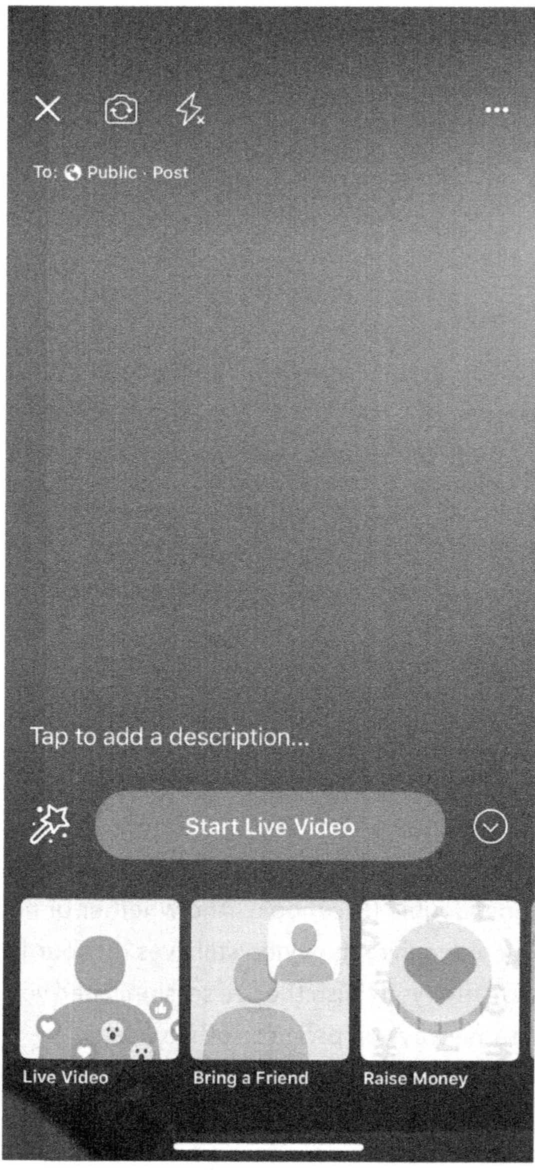

Keep in mind that live videos take a lot of preparation. Before you go live, make sure you have your 'scene' set up. If you are going to be moving around, you will want a clear path and a plan. You will also need to have a loose plan as to what you are going to cover in your video. The reason we say loose is because so much of what makes live video captivating is the interaction with the audience. Live video is a stream shown to people in real time. People who tune in are able to comment and interact with both the creator and the other members. That's what makes live so appealing to viewers—when done correctly, they get to take part in the narrative.

Have a fully charged phone before going live. Go to your Page on your Facebook app and tap the "Publish" icon. Your screen will now have a place to type at the top and a bunch of suggested actions. Choose "Live Video."

Your Facebook Live screen is now up on your phone, but don't worry, you aren't live yet. Before you actually go live, write a short description about what you are going to be talking about. As soon as you're ready and set up, you just have to tap "Start Live Video" and your post (and video) will go live. The second you go live, and for a bit afterwards, Facebook will send push notifications to people who follow your page and it will notify them if they log into Facebook while you're live. Facebook *wants* people to tune into your live video.

When You're Live

Once you go live, share the stream to your Facebook Page and encourage people to tune in and share the stream as well. This is one of those times when it may be worth having someone else working with you while doing your video. In the marketing industry, they are called community managers. This person could be your assistant, a spouse, or even a virtual assistant.

As people start to tune in, there are a few best practices to follow:

- Greet people by their name as they tune in
- Ask questions of the audience

- Repeat the questions people are asking in the comments and then answer them
- State who asked the question before answering it
- Check in with the audience periodically
- Be willing to get "off topic" to better serve the audience

Are you sensing a theme? A good livestream revolves around the audience and the interaction between the creator and the audience.

Remember, you are always on camera and people can see everything! Don't walk past the dirty laundry, make sure you don't have kiddos coming in and interrupting every five minutes and, like we talked about in Chapter 5, ensure great lighting no matter where you go.

Using Live as a Strategy

Focus on two strategies for Facebook Live: series and open houses. A Facebook Live series is very personal and should run either bi-weekly or monthly. Your series should cover conversational topics (like common home selling questions) in a relaxed environment. Or do a series with guests who talk about different real estate focused topics where you feed the guests questions live from the audience.

The other strategy for live video is virtual open houses. These can be done either in conjunction with or instead of in-person open houses, but they offer similar(ish) opportunities to the audience. A live virtual open house will allow viewers to ask to see the things that mean the most to them and give their thoughts as you take them around the house. The value to you, the agent, is that you can control the audience' view. While showing the things people want to see, you're able to speak to them through their entire experience of "walking" through the house as you show things in their best light. These open houses also help the audience because they don't have to leave their house or feel the pressure of having an agent following them around, so they may be more likely to attend a virtual open house.

Facebook Events

The absolute best part of Facebook Live, no matter which strategy you are using, is you can create Facebook events to promote them. Facebook events are invaluable to event hosts because if people note they are interested, Facebook will send them reminders as the event nears. Events also provide another platform to gather input from the audience before you go live.

Setting up a quality Facebook event for livestream can be done on your phone or computer. Go to your Facebook Page and the place where you usually go to post. Once you click into that screen, select "create an event." To create an event, you will need an event title, an event graphic, and a description. Each follows the same rules as for other videos, the only difference is that the event graphic should be 1.91:1 or 1260 x 656. Like we said in Chapter 10, Canva is a great place to create graphics like this.

Set it up about seven to ten days before your event. After you create the event on your Facebook page (you guessed it) share it to your Facebook profile. You should also share it on your other social profiles and even in your email newsletters as the events will have immediate value. This ensures people who want to attend know in advance the time and date and can be prepared to log in.

Smart Tip: Use the list of people who attended or showed interest in your event to target them later with Facebook ads!

Chapter 12

Instagram

Learn why Instagram is where your current and future clients are and how they want to connect through stories, Instagram Live, and video feeds.

Instagram is the up and coming platform for adults. From 2014-2019, the percentage of all adults eighteen and older using Instagram went from sixteen to thirty-seven percent (Pew Research Center). As more adults move over to Instagram, the value of this platform rises for Realtors®. Gone are the days of using Instagram to get "likes" on overly edited photos of million-dollar houses that the majority of people "liking" them could never afford. There is far more buying power on Instagram today, and a greater ability to reach those who are actively interested in purchasing a home.

Instagram is owned by Facebook and the algorithms are a bit similar. Much like Facebook, Instagram favors video, as videos get more interaction. If you search #realestate on Instagram, you'll find very few Realtors® have started using video. This is a massive opportunity for you to get a head start!

The platform is very unique though and it requires a little bit of love affection. While you can easily use the same square videos Facebook on your Instagram and get decent results, you won't to get away with only using those.

Four Major Types of Video on Instagram:

Videos in the Feed

On the Instagram app, the photos and videos you've recently taken will pop up when you click the plus sign in the middle of the bottom navigation. From there, select a video you want to post. However, keep in mind that these posts are only able to show one minute of video at a time.

This leaves you with two options if your video is longer than a minute: you can either split the video into one minute chunks and post them in a carousel, or you can post the video as an IGTV segment (more on that in a minute). If you want to post your video in one-minute segments in a carousel, your video will have to be less than ten minutes (which it should be so as not to lose viewers' attention) as Instagram only allows up to ten items in a carousel. You will need to prompt people to scroll through the video carousel as most will not do so intuitively.

It's smart to stick to one video that is sixty seconds or less. These posts can be brief testimonials, quicks tips, or a sneak peek of a house you ˈave listed. Also, much like Facebook, square videos perform very well ... Instagram feed, so you can crop your video into a square or edit ... ˈe same way as the Facebook square videos.

... relatively new addition to the Instagram ... out in June of 2018. IGTV is a place for ... —these videos can be up to sixty ... your computer. From your ... videos.

... artphone or from your ... slightly between the two. ... ione is the same process as uploading a regular video on your phone, except before you hit "next" you have to specify whether you want to upload the long video to IGTV or share up to one minute of your video. This process is a bit different on your computer, however. To upload an IGTV video on your computer, you must go to your profile, select "IGTV" from the section under your bio and then select "upload." A screen will populate that shows you all of the options you have when uploading an IGTV video. Much like Facebook, write a catchy title and a short description of what the video is about. Choose a cover that will stand out on the feed or you can even upload one that you create. Think of it as a thumbnail except it should be 1:1.55 or 420 x 654 px.

Smart Tip: The recommended cover size is a sign from Instagram that IGTV videos should be taken and posted in a vertical format.

Check the "post a preview" box to post the video to your feed, which will be shown as a one-minute clip. Make sure that minute is engaging! Once the minute is up, viewers will see a screen encouraging them to "Keep Watching." If they select that button, they will be taken to a full screen experience where they can watch the rest of the video.

These videos should be high value, giving people invaluable advice or showing high entertainment value. For real estate agents, our advice is to stick to adding value through educational tips. Entertaining people can be tough.

2. Instagram Stories

An Instagram story is a fifteen-second video that lives for twenty-four hours, creating intrigue and buzz, because as soon as the content arrives—it disappears!

But not really. You (not your viewers) always have the ability to view the stories you've previously posted by going to your Instagram Profile on your phone, pressing the three lines in the top right hand corner and selecting "Archives." You can also add your stories to your profile *Highlights* by viewing the story and selecting "Highlight." Add the story to an existing Highlight or create a new Highlight. To see good examples of Highlights, visit the profile @yourphoenixhomegirl.

Stories should be quick and exciting! Your audience has only twenty-four hours to view them (if you choose) so this is the place to let loose a bit. Go behind the scenes, show yourself being silly, post bloopers from a new video, share breaking news, just have fun.

To post an Instagram story, open the Instagram app on your phone and click your profile picture in the top left corner. Your camera will open, and you will be ready to start recording. But before you start recording, note the orientation of the camera—it's vertical! You'll want to keep that in mind when preparing to shoot. When you hold down the video button to record, you will not be stopped at fifteen seconds, instead Instagram automatically starts the next video for you if you go over fifteen seconds. It's recommended to post no more than sixty seconds at a time.

Once posted, these videos will only be viewable by users if they tap on your profile icon at the top of their feed or in the middle of their feed, and don't worry, they will. Stats show that over 500 million users view Instagram stories every day.[12]

Smart Tip: If you want to post more than one set of Instagram stories in a day, simply tap the blue plus sign under your profile picture on either your home or profile page.

3. Instagram Live

Instagram Live is much like Facebook Live without the ability to invite people via events. Going live on Instagram sends out notifications to your followers and pushes your icon towards the beginning of people's story roll. Start by going to the same place you would go to create a story, but instead of taking a video story, you will scroll the little menu on the bottom of the screen from "normal" to "live."

Smart Tip: Live is the last option all the way to the left.

Once you are live, Instagram will start notifying your followers and try to get them to join in. When they join, greet them by name and start engaging with them. Instagram Live is a bit more interactive as people can request to go live with you and they can also submit questions via question cards you can post on your story. Both of these options are great ways to get your audience involved in your stream, however, you should only use these features when they make sense. Don't just let anyone go live with you and only allow people to submit questions (by tapping the two squares with a question mark on it when you're live) when it's a situation that calls for questions - like open houses.

Remember, live video should be reserved for topics or instances where you are willing to involve the audience. Otherwise, you should stick to stories or IGTV.

---

[12] Newberry, Christina. "37 Instagram Statistics That Matter to Marketers in 2020." October 22, 2019. https://blog.hootsuite.com/instagram-statistics/.

Promoting Your Instagram Content

Instagram is a tough market to break into, but if you follow a few key tips, you will have some good strategies to help you get started.

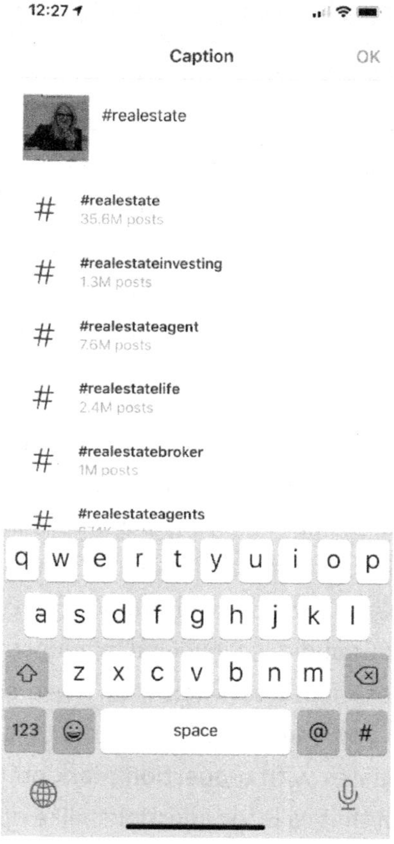

Hashtags

Always use hashtags on Instagram. When you upload a video to your feed, to IGTV, or as a story, you will be able to add hashtags. In the feed and on IGTV, add hashtags in the description. These hashtags should be specific to what you talk about in your video. When you are posting from your phone, as you start to type in a hashtag, Instagram will show you suggestions with a count showing how many times the hashtag has been used.

The ideal setup for your hashtags is two or three that have a lot of posts and three to five hashtags that don't (less than 500K). This strategy evens out your chances of being seen. Some of those smaller hashtags should be specific to the town or city you serve. These tags may be harder to find, but they will generate more valuable views and potential leads.

To be seen, add hashtags to your stories. To do this, select the hashtag sticker after you are done recording your video by going to the edit screen with eight icons across the top. Tap the fifth icon from the left; it will have a smiley face in a square with the bottom right corner folded in. Choose the sticker that says "HASHTAG." Hashtags make you more discoverable, so use one or two hashtags in your stories and ensure they are local.

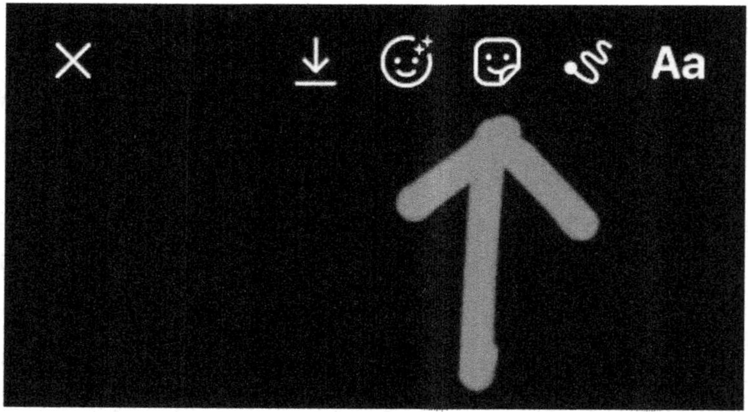

Location Tags

A lot of searches are done by location. Using location tags can increase your visibility within your local community.

Location tags are exactly what they sound like, they are a tag of where you were when you took your video. When you upload a video to Instagram, you are asked to "Add a Location," with some auto-generated suggestions. If you want to tag a different location, simply tap the "Add a Location" section and type in an address.

If you took a video at a house you are showing, you can tag the city or even the neighborhood, but you won't be able to tag the actual address.

Chapter 13

LinkedIn

Find potential buyers on LinkedIn and learn how it's a video marketer's untapped space

LinkedIn is full of potential buyers. According to Pew Research, almost half of all U.S. adults who make over $75,000 a year are on LinkedIn.[13] LinkedIn users are educated, older, and financially stable—pretty ideal for Realtors®! LinkedIn rolled out video on their platform in 2017 and few people have figured it out, making it a video marketer's dream. LinkedIn could be your sweet spot.

LinkedIn videos can be uploaded to the platform on either mobile or desktop. They can also be embedded from places like YouTube to create a look and feel similar to YouTube embeds on Facebook.

Uploading Videos to LinkedIn

Videos on LinkedIn must be at least three seconds long and no longer than ten minutes. Videos will upload straight into a post where all you will have to do is write your post and add your hashtags. For your description, you will want the first two lines to tell people what the video is about, but also keep them wanting more. Then you should list the high points using emojis or bullet points.

---

[13] Perrin, Andrew, and Monica Anderson. "Share of U.S. Adults Using Social Media, including Facebook, Is Mostly Unchanged since 2018." April 10, 2019. https://www.pewresearch.org/fact-tank/2019/04/10/share-of-u-s-adults-using-social-media-including-facebook-is-mostly-unchanged-since-2018/.

It's DRIVING ME NUTS

How can you look at the SAME accounts every day? ...see more

18 · 5 Comments · 684 Views

Brie E Anderson
An Analytical Nerd with a Soft Spot for Strategy | SEO Geek
6mo ·

It's DRIVING ME NUTS

How can you look at the SAME accounts every day?

And think that you are TRULY getting them to their highest potential?

Without having COMPLETELY FRESH eyes on them?

You need to have your ads, landing pages, strategies, etc reviewed AT LEAST quarterly

Or you are doing a disservice to your clients

#marketing #socialmediamarketing #socialmedia #strategies #seo #digitalmarketing #marketingstrategy #business #businesstruths

After you add your description, end it with some hashtags, ideally three or four, but there is no limit. Hashtags should be specific to what you talk about in your video. People follow specific hashtags which increases your chances of being seen by customers seeking your content.

Upload from Your Phone

On your iPhone, tap the plus sign in the circle box at the bottom of the screen and select the icon that looks like a photo. This will pull up your entire camera roll of photos and videos, and from here you can select the video you want to upload. Once your video uploads, just tap the arrow icon in the bottom right corner. The video will now be in your post.

Upload from Your Computer

Uploading from your computer is pretty similar to uploading from your phone. The difference is once you get to the box to upload your video instead of seeing a picture icon to select, you will see a video camera icon. Once you select that icon, your computer files will show up and you can select the file that you want to upload. A screen will pop up asking if you want to "Edit" the video, the functionalities here are limited and there is nothing here that can add value, so just select "done."

After your videos are loaded in the post and you've added your descriptions and hashtags, it's time to set the post free!

Smart Tip: Make sure your posts are set to "Public."

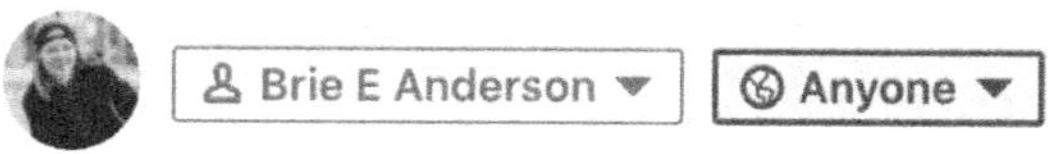

Embedding YouTube Videos into LinkedIn Posts

Just like on your Facebook page, you can embed your YouTube video in your LinkedIn post by copying and pasting the YouTube link into your LinkedIn post. After a second or two, LinkedIn will generate the thumbnail and title of your YouTube video. Once this preview is generated, you can safely remove the link from your post and the video and thumbnail will remain.

LinkedIn, unlike Facebook, does not heavily punish you for embedding videos this way. There may be a slight decrease in reach, but as long as you can get engagement on your post, your reach will be just fine.

Post YouTube videos on LinkedIn within 24 hours of the video going live so people will click on the video and view it, therefore increasing the view time of your video on YouTube and increasing the interaction rate on your LinkedIn post. A double-whammy!

LinkedIn Video Best Practices

Posting on LinkedIn is not as difficult as other platforms. LinkedIn content lives for about a week without you actively promoting your video, and this provides engagement and views for that full week. On other platforms, content will die within a day or even hours, depending on when, where, and how you post. As long as people have interacted with your videos in the past, LinkedIn will ensure they see your future videos the next time they log on. This is because LinkedIn users are different from average social media users, as most LinkedIn users only log in one or fewer times a day (statistically). That said, if people comment on your video you should reply as soon as possible to catch them before they log off for the day. The best way to do this is to be sure you have your notifications on.

Posting one or two videos a week is plenty, again because most people don't get fresh content in their feed as they aren't logging on enough to trigger LinkedIn to show new content. Instead, LinkedIn shows content they assume users will interact with most.

The best times to post are first thing in the morning or at lunch time, but it is not imperative you post at those exact times. Only post videos in landscape orientation, as this is how they show up in the feed.

What Content to Post

LinkedIn video is still a mystery because LinkedIn is a business to business platform, which is very different from every other social platform. LinkedIn weighs content by considering the three main reasons people use the platform: employment, networking, and learning.

How can you create video that helps a viewer achieve those things while also getting them closer to buying a property?

Education

Well, education is the easy option. Offer expert advice on how to get more for your property, how to choose properties, how to lower your mortgage payment, etc. When you look at all of those topics, they have one thing in common—money. People on LinkedIn aspire to be greater than what they already are and a major part of that is having more money. Find ways to educate them about money and real estate and then, when they are ready to buy or sell, they will want to reach out to you because you're an expert.

Also, talk business! Talk about processes you have that work. Talk about how you sell. Talk about lessons you've learned. Business is a skill everyone can get better at and business is what everyone on LinkedIn understands. Don't be so focused on trying to sell or push your business, instead share what you've learned. When people are ready to buy or sell, you will be top of mind.

Networking

A fun way to encourage networking on your LinkedIn videos is to introduce the different teams you work with and have them tell their stories. Interview a loan officer and ask them what kind of education they needed to have, what their journey was to get the job, how long they've been doing it, why it's important people use them, and what kind of business they handle outside of mortgages. These kinds of interviews are great for three reasons:

- They give people an idea of who you do business with,
- They get your team in front of other potential clients, and
- They give your audience people to network with and potentially do business with in the future.

LinkedIn can be a valuable platform if used correctly. Don't be afraid to try a few different styles of videos and replicate the ones that perform best.

Chapter 14

Video and Email Marketing

Email marketing is one of the oldest, most effective forms of digital marketing. Even with the increase in spam filters and folders, almost sixty percent of marketers claim email is their biggest source of return on investment.[14] The best thing about email marketing is that it doesn't have to be terribly difficult.

Many businesses send out email newsletters, some two or three times a week. Some businesses only send out sales announcements. How do you think those work out? Think about how well that goes over—probably not well as the clients will inevitably get annoyed and unsubscribe.

The Secret to Email Marketing

Emails should go out no more than once a week and they should be extremely relevant to the audience. The best way to do this is by segmenting your email list. Some email platforms allow you to do this automatically based on how the contact is added to your list or through the choices the contact selects when they sign up, but almost all platforms allow you to hand select and tag contacts. This process, while tedious, will have a major impact on your bottom line.

According to Campaign Monitor, marketers saw a 760 percent increase in return on investment when they segmented their lists.[15] List

---

[14] Forsey, Caroline. "The Ultimate List of Email Marketing Stats for 2020." February 26, 2020. https://blog.hubspot.com/marketing/email-marketing-stats.
[15] "New Rules of Email Marketing [2019]."
https://www.campaignmonitor.com/resources/guides/email-marketing-new-rules/.

segments are done in many ways, but for real estate professionals, these are some general segmentation rules:

- Buyers
  - Town
  - Budget range
  - First time vs repeat buyer
- Sellers
  - Town
- General / Miscellaneous

Knowing and storing this information allows you to create automated email campaigns that keep your client in the loop and push them down the funnel all at once.

Adding video to an email can increase the click-through rate over 300 percent.[16] That means over 300 percent more clicks will go to your website because you introduced video.

Best Practices

As much as video may help your email campaign, it can do the opposite if you don't do it correctly. Instead of attaching a video, add it in the body of the email. This requires embedding the video or adding a photo with a play button into the email and linking that image to a video player that opens in another tab.

To embed the video in the email, use a platform like Bomb Bomb, Wistia or Vidyard. Each of those platforms host videos on their websites and then serve them to your clients through your emails. Refer to their help

---

[16] Nottingham, "Your Business's Videos Should Include Faces. Here's Why," Wistia.

pages to learn about their integrations with your email marketing platform.

To bypass the need for a separate platform, upload an image to your email and hyperlink it to a webpage that houses the video. If you decide to do this, it's recommended that you send the viewer to a page on your website with the video on it. We will cover what that might look like in the next chapter.

Make sure the email subject line notes that there is a video in the email. This can increase your open rate by almost twenty percent.[17] It's common to see [VIDEO] at the end of the subject line of an email with an enclosed video.

Ex: "3 EASY ways to increase your home value 🤑[Video]"

Lastly, remember that people check their email at crazy times or at work. That being said, ensure that you are only using video when you *need* to in order to give the most value. Also, make sure to add captions (closed or opened) so viewers can watch the video even if they can't hear the sound (see our recommendations in Chapter 10 on how to add captions) because they are at work or somewhere inappropriate to play sounds out loud.

[17] Forsey, "The Ultimate List of Email Marketing Stats for 2020," Hubspot.

Strategies for Buyers

Set up different email campaigns for first-time and repeat buyers because the needs of these groups are very different.

First-time buyers will need a series of educational videos. A few suggestions include:

1. **Introduction** "Thanks for your interest in working with me on your home buying journey. I am here for any questions you have, etc." This video should be no longer than sixty seconds.
2. **What's the Home Buying Process?** Talk about the typical process and how you fit into that process. This video may be a bit long but shouldn't be any longer than three minutes. In this email, be sure to offer a phone call, meeting at the office, meeting at buyer's home, or a Zoom meeting.
3. **What to Know When Buying a House.** Talk about some of the things that first-time homebuyers don't expect. A short video, no longer than thirty seconds, would work well in this type of email.
4. **Showings- Why to Go and What to See.** Show a sample home listing with your voiceover explaining specific things to look for in a home. At the end of this video, offer to take the potential buyer on a showing, or list some of your upcoming open houses.

After this series of emails, additional emails should be listing-specific and more personalized. Not every email needs to have a video, but when you are trying to show your value as a Realtor®, a few videos can help a potential buyer learn to trust your face and voice. As you build a relationship with your potential client, you can start to send personalized videos where you call them by name and address their specific concerns and needs.

For repeat buyers, depending on their wants and needs, offer tips on "buying your forever home" or "what to look for in a retirement home."

Like first-time buyers, the introductory phase for repeat buyers involves gaining trust. Start with an introduction video and then a video on "what it's like to buy a house with (insert your/brokerage name here)." The potential buyer may know what it is like to buy a house, but you should share why working with you is different and valuable.

Repeat buyers are more likely to know what they want, so personalize their experience sooner than a first-time home buyer. Don't be afraid to send those personalized videos within the first two weeks to show that you are dedicated to helping them find their perfect property.

Strategies for Sellers

People looking to sell a house are likely looking for one of two things—the biggest payout or the quickest turn around. If you can find out which kind of seller you are working with right away, it will be easier to tailor the messages, but if you don't know, offer information on both possibilities.

Here's some ideas for an email educational series for sellers using video:

1. **Introduction** "Thanks for your interest in working with me on your selling journey. I am here for any questions you have, etc." This video should be no longer than sixty seconds.
2. **What's the selling process?** Talk about the typical process and how you fit into that process, where money is made and how time is spent. This video may be a bit long but shouldn't be any longer than three minutes. In this email, be sure to offer a phone call, meeting at the sellers' home, or a Zoom meeting.
3. **What to know when selling a house.** Talk about some of the things people don't expect when selling a house.

4. **Showings - how to hold one**. This doesn't need to be a video, but it can be. Show visuals of good versus bad showings and an itinerary of what setting up a showing may look like.

5. **How closings work for a seller.** Talk about where money can be gained or lost and where things can go wrong or take extra time. This video may be a bit longer, but again don't go over three minutes. At the end, encourage them to schedule a call with you.

Adjust and edit these videos as they make sense for your business, but always keep in mind the needs of the seller. After all, it's all about them!

General

Your email list will also include people you know nothing about, or those who are former clients with whom you want to stay in touch.

This group is perfect to include in your weekly or bi-weekly newsletter. Whether they are buyers, sellers, prospects or former clients, everyone on your email list can benefit from content written for a general audience interested in real estate. A biweekly newsletter can highlight all of the content you are creating. Show some of your new listings and highlight a neighborhood.

When it comes to newsletters the biggest rule is: BE CONSISTENT. Send weekly or biweekly and have a template that you follow. A sample template could include:

- A featured piece of content
- Any new listings
- One happy client (buyer or seller)
- Seller's tip of the week
- Neighborhood of the month video highlighting something cool

The above template is filled with content that can interest buyers, sellers, and anyone else who might just be your next client.

Chapter 15

Using Video on Your Website

Video can enhance your real estate website to make your website actively market for you.

Now that you have a variety of engaging and educational videos, it's time to showcase them in your digital house—your website! Similar to email, video on your website can produce real results when done correctly, but if they aren't used strategically, it can have the opposite result.

By hosting website video on YouTube, this will take some of the "weight" of the video off of your website and will transfer that over to YouTube - this makes your website load much quicker. Putting a YouTube video on your website is easy too. Some website builders have premade widgets that allow you to just drop the YouTube link in the widget to embed the video. For all other website builders, use the html code YouTube generates. To do this, go to your YouTube video, select "share," and then select "embed." From there you just copy the code, go back to your website builder and paste the code in the section where you want it to show up.

Something to keep in mind when putting these videos on your website is that you never want a video to autoplay with the sound on. This can scare and/or annoy people and they will leave. When people quickly leave your website over and over again, this tells search engines like Google that something is wrong and that will discourage them from showing your page in the search results.

Introduction Videos

The one video you've heard about over and again throughout this book is your introduction video. Truly, everyone should have an introduction video. Place this video on your profile page on your brokerage website. Or, if you have your own website, it could live on your home page. No matter where the video lives, you will not want it to autoplay. You will want the viewer to show initiative and press the play button. If they press play, it's reasonable they will want to spend sixty seconds getting to know you.

Client Testimonials

The next place that should, without a doubt, have videos is your client testimonials page (or section). A written testimonial is one thing, but as we've learned already, the power of a face builds far more trust and interest. Plus, with a video testimonial, the viewer gets to see those non-verbal cues that allow the viewer to put themselves in the shoes of the client.

Admittedly, these videos can be a bit tough to capture, as most people aren't a huge fan of taking videos, but you are in sales after all! One of the best ways to get a client testimonial video is to make it as easy as possible. If you are doing a closing at the office, have the equipment set up and assume they will say yes to recording right then and there. You can also encourage people to record their own testimonials at home and email them to you - this would obviously be an instance where you won't use *every* video that comes in, but that you could get more engagement. Sometimes you can raffle something off to people to give testimonials, but you can't always do that because then it's bribery! The biggest piece of advice for securing these testimonials is to just make it EASY.

When it comes to client testimonial videos, the videos should *only* have the client in them. Ideally, you would have a mix of professionally produced and personalized videos. Professional testimonials will show your credentials and be one of the first testimonials people see. The personalized testimonial videos are for the more skeptical future clients. Personalized client testimonials may be videos that your previous clients take at their new property or it could be a video you take for them right after you hand them their check. These videos are going to be far more powerful than the prompted professional videos, but they will likely look less polished (again, less polished can also mean more authentic). It's smart to have a mix of the two.

If you have a single page of client testimonials, work with a web developer to make sure the page is optimized for speed as you will have several videos embedded on it which can slow down their play quality. If you are placing testimonials throughout your site, make sure to have no more than two or three videos on a page. Not only can it slow your site, it can signal to Google not to send people to the pages because the users may have a bad experience.

Listings

Another no-brainer place for videos to live is on your listing pages. If you have professionally shot footage of your property, make sure to attach a short introduction video. If you don't have footage, use the video lessons (remember the gimbal?) from chapter three and get your own footage. Either way, make sure that there is a ten-second video of you introducing yourself as the agent. This short clip should play before the listing video kicks in.

Live Streams

A really cool feature of Facebook Live streams is the ability to embed the live stream on your website. Using your computer, go to your Facebook Page and in the top navigation select "Creator Studio." If it is not there for you, you can navigate to "More" > "Publishing Tools" and then find "Creator Studio" on the left.

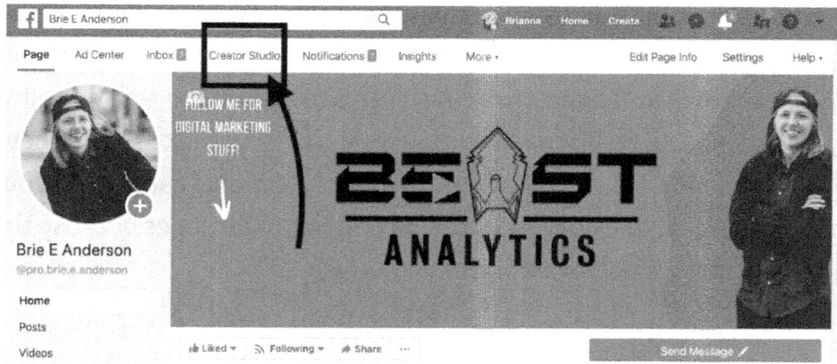

Once you are in Creator Studio, select "create post" in the top left corner. When the dropdown appears select "Go live." A new tab will open. In this new tab, look to the top left and select "Schedule a Live Video."

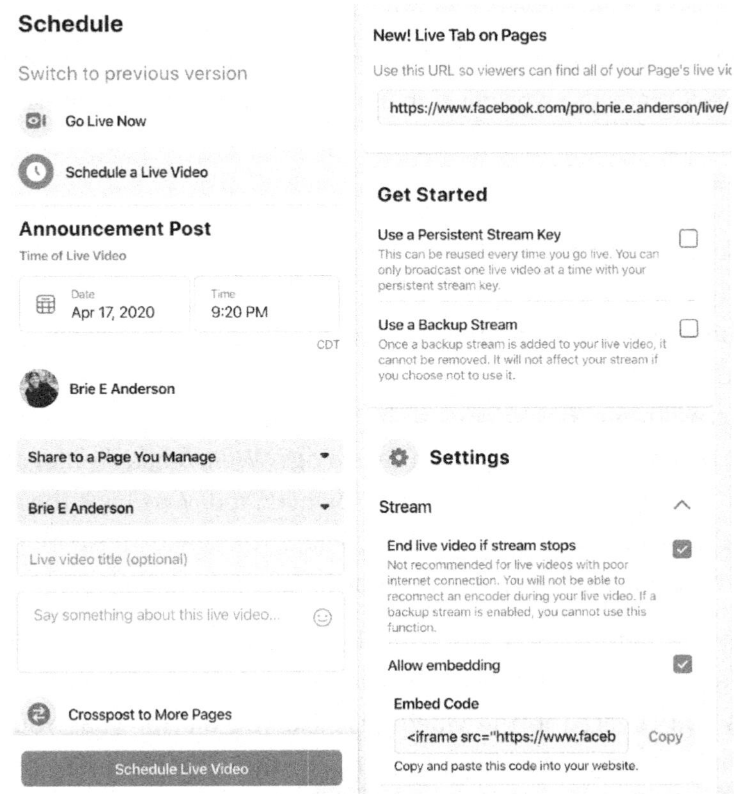

Once you've selected "schedule a live video" your page will change. Select the date you want to livestream and write a description for the video. Most importantly, in the "settings" section, click the downward facing arrow across from "stream" to find an embed code.

Facebook will automatically show these lives as they happen, but you can also embed them onto your website. Copy the embed code from Creator Studio so that you can paste it onto a page where you want to live stream to be shown. Ideally, you would schedule these live streams for your virtual open houses and then embed the streams onto the listing pages of the houses that will be showing.

To take this strategy a step further, you could even put an event on the listing page people could save to their phone with the location set to your webpage. This will remind them to come back to your site to see your virtual open house. **Just note** - this is a bit more advanced and may require contacting a web developer or your internal IT/ marketing team.

Blogs

The number one way to drive new traffic to your website is to have a blog. Your website's blog should answer a lot of questions people would ask about your business. And if it does, and it does a good job, Google will put it high in the search results. Plus, if it answers questions well, people will refer their friends to it, too! That's a lot of new clients to reach, so why don't more people have blogs? Well, originally blogs were all text based. In fact, some still are. However, today we have the ability to add images and, you guessed it, video, to blogs. These elements make blogs far more interesting for both readers and creators.

Once you create a video, you are halfway done with a blog post. Now, write a short three-sentence introduction and create a list of the main things you covered in the video, just like you did for your YouTube description, except that they should not be the exact same description. Then add a few more words in your blog post. Another option is to transcribe your video and then format it into a blog post. You can easily hire someone to do this for very little cost.

After you've written your blog post, it's time to get it up on your website. Now, there is a very specific structure you are going to want to use, so pay close attention and be sure to share this with your website person!

- The title of your video (this will be the largest heading on the page and the title of the blog post).
- The two or three sentences you wrote as your introduction.
- Your embedded YouTube video.

- The rest of the blog post follows the video.

After a YouTube video goes live, wait roughly twenty-four to forty-eight hours before posting the blog post. This allows the blog posts to give your YouTube video a second wave of interactions and views.

Chapter 16

Start Building Your Video Library

People want to do business with people they know, like, and trust. It helps put their minds at ease by lessening the risk, and at least one of the unknowns. People want to know that you won't steer them wrong, especially with buying and selling homes and property—major decisions that can affect their entire lives. They need to be able to trust your intention, your reliability, your sincerity, and to know that you are easy to work with.

For potential clients who are looking for an agent, video is a way for them to get to know you and build trust. For people who know you, it reinforces what they already thought, that you are the expert! Video allows potential clients to visualize how you do business, how you think, and what it will be like working with you. A video library is the visual display of your knowledge and expertise. Through videos, you can educate, inform, earn trust, and keep the respect of current and future clients.

A well-made, thoughtful video library can allow people to get to know you, to like you, and to trust you. The following are a few strategies on how to get people to know, like, and trust you through videos.

To Know You

Let your personality show through. Choose three things you wish to convey about yourself (i.e. reliable, personable, caring). Write scripts that demonstrate these traits. Rather than stating to people, "I am reliable," *tell* them a story of how you were reliable in a relevant situation. Focus on showing a sense of being personable or caring. Share a story about how you make friends wherever you go and give a specific example. Share the reasons you care about helping people buy and sell homes and properties.

To Like You

In order to like you, people must feel they connect with you. This can be through shared values, a shared sense of humor, shared interests, or how you make them feel. This is where you can shine in your videos. Show people who you are, and they will get to know you and like you. This isn't about becoming best friends, but invoking that feeling that makes someone think, "I like this person." You know *that* feeling.

Create videos that make people feel good about you and the prospect of working with you. Use second-person language and speak directly to people in the videos. *Do you feel like you have gotten to know me a little through reading this book?* It's more personal and increases the sense of connection. Avoid using sales jargon. Make genuine and useful videos such as "how tos," "step-by-steps," and "checklists." Most of all, be honest, open, and be who you are--your values and interests will naturally come through.

To Trust You

To trust someone in business, you must feel comfortable. You want to anticipate and feel good about the likelihood of how this professional will behave and conduct themselves while doing business with you. Through videos you can help clients trust your work ethic, your attention to detail, and your commitment to helping them find and buy or sell their homes and property.

When you make a video with accurate, reliable information, it builds trust. When you explain a process in a video, and then follow up with the client as promised—it builds trust. Through testimonial videos, you provide social proof that you are trustworthy. People are more likely to trust you when you've already been vetted by others they relate to.

A video library will make you more efficient. Work or parenting schedules make it difficult to connect with clients. Being able to send your clients a video about whatever part of the process you're in allows you to answer their questions at their convenience *and yours*!

The ultimate goal is for you to have an entire library of videos answering every question that comes up in your real estate business. But you may find it easier to start with the basics. Below is a list of the first nine videos you should focus on. Once finished, you can build from there.

Here are nine videos every agent needs in their video library:

1. **A professional introductory video.** A real estate introductory video should be informal; a quick, friendly video to introduce yourself to cold leads online, as well as warmer leads who may want to get to know you better. Focus on who you are as a person and how you will add value to the home buying/selling experience. Be creative and use your personal interests, affiliations, and hobbies to solidify your commitment and familiarity with the local community.

2. **A professional testimonial video from your clients**. Testimonial videos are heartfelt and feel more genuine than written reviews which can be written by anyone. People trust video testimonials much more than written ones. Consider adding a testimonial video or two into your introductory video. These can be informal and should be genuine.

3. **A professional or pre-recorded video about the community you serve**. This video establishes you as the authority in the community. Give a brief overview of the community along with known landmarks or popular places, a brief descriptor of the people (friendly, hardworking, relaxed, etc.), and what you love about living and serving there. This video will help the people who live in the community feel a sense of

connection with you and will help people relocating become familiar with you and the area.

You should create at least three videos for buyers answering commonly asked questions, such as:

4. How much can I afford?
5. What are the steps in buying a home?
6. How do I make an offer on a house?

You should create at least three videos for sellers answering commonly asked questions, such as:

7. What are the steps in selling a home?
8. What should I do to get my house ready to sell?
9. What is a comparative market analysis?

There are countless evergreen videos you can create. These are just a few to get you started with building a foundation. In the next chapters, you will find a list of over fifty video ideas and a Blueprint for Video Success.

Chapter 17

50+ Video Ideas

Get started building your own video library with ideas, tips, and inspiration.

Here's a list of essential videos for your real estate video library:

Introductory Video

Client Testimonial

City/Community Video

Buyer Videos

- How much can I afford
- Pre-approval process
- What to look for when buying a home
- Explaining Zillow and other online resources
- Making an offer
- What happens to earnest money?
- Escalation clauses/multiple offers
- Writing a contingent offer
- Looking at houses (show a walk-through)
- Different types of financing
    - FHA
    - VA
    - Insured Conventional
    - Conventional

- Closing costs
- Can I buy a car or furniture before closing?
- Appraisal
- Title work
- What is title insurance and why do I need it?
- Do I need a home warranty?
- What to expect at closing

Seller videos

- Market analysis
- Pre-inspection
- Staging your house
- Filling out disclosures
- Tips for interviewing real estate agents
- Explaining Zillow and other online resources
- Do I really need to take down my pictures?
- Do I really need to get rid of one-third of my stuff?
- Showing your house
- Open houses
- What to do when you receive an offer
- Negotiating an offer
- What to expect during an inspection
- Appraisal
- Preparing for closing
- The walk-through
- Dealing with pets during showings

- Smoke smells and pet odors
- Dealing with feedback

Interviews with other professionals

- Inspector
- Loan officer
- Appraiser
- Stager
- Design tips
- Home maintenance
- Electrician
- Plumber
- Roofer
- HVAC
- Contractors

Town/Neighborhood Expert

- Visit local shops
- Restaurants
- Schools
- Parks
- Landmarks
- Why people like living in the neighborhood
- History of your city
- Major employers

Highlight Special Events in Town

- Festivals
- Charity Events
- Holiday Events

News events that affect real estate

- Interest rates
- Inman news
- Realtor® Magazine

Weather related tips for selling real estate

- Snow: Shovel walks, roofs, etc.
- Scorching heat: Keep the house cool, etc.
- Rain: Keep an umbrella and rug by the front door

Chapter 18

The Blueprint to Success

You've been given the keys to the kingdom. You know what kind of videos to create, how to create them, and where to put them. Chances are, you're starting to freak out about figuring out how the heck you are going to get started on all of this. Fear not. Here's your Blueprint to Success: the entire process broken down into a manageable process.

Step 1: Create a Production Schedule

Most people will take a day and shoot as many videos as possible. Because most of the videos are short, if you set up to shoot for a half a day, you could get close to a month's worth of personalized / professional content done in a day. If a half day of shooting does not seem feasible or fun to do once a month, shoot for an hour or so every week. Either way, you need to account for about **four hours of video shoot a month for professional/personalized videos** that will go on your YouTube, Facebook, Instagram, and LinkedIn feeds as well as on your website. You could also use this time to create the videos you will need for emails.

Smart Tip: There will be times that you have to record at the last minute. There will be times when you *should* record at the last minute and that is okay! This schedule is the best-case scenario.

Step 2: Create a Post-Production Schedule

After recording all of your videos, it's time to edit. For every minute of video you record, you should schedule two to three minutes of post-production work.

During post-production you will:

- Edit your videos
- Make ten-to thirty-second preview videos for promotion
- Write the titles
- Write descriptions
- Write the blog posts
- Create the thumbnails
- Schedule the videos

If you shoot once a month, you can either schedule a full day of editing every month or break it down to an hour or so for every three days of editing.

Step 3: Create a Sharing Schedule

Day #1: If you use YouTube, this strategy is going to be rather easy. You will publish one YouTube video every week. Post a link to the YouTube video on your Facebook Page and your LinkedIn. Then share your Facebook Page post to your Facebook Profile.

Day #2: Make a blog post that covers the topic of your video and embed the YouTube video in that post. Publish the blog post on your website.

Day #3: Post the square promo videos to your Facebook, LinkedIn, and Instagram feeds.

Day #7: Either link to the blog post or feature your video in your email newsletter.

Day #10: Post the entire video (not just the link) directly on Facebook, LinkedIn, and IGTV.

Day #14: Share a link to your blog post about the YouTube video on Facebook and LinkedIn.

Smart Tip: Once you start posting regularly, switch this up a bit to better fit your schedule or because you notice that some things work and others don't. That is normal. You will also notice that the majority of the content you will need for social media and email will be done in a flash because you will have video-related content to share almost every day.

Bonus Tip: Don't forget about the videos you create—share them! Sometimes a video will answer a question you will likely get in the future. Don't be afraid to answer a future question today with a link to a YouTube video. Don't be afraid to produce a quick video to answer a complex question for a client. These video answers can be extremely helpful to clients and will earn you massive brownie points.

VIDEO SHARING SCHEDULE

DAY 1
Publish YouTube Video. Post YouTube link on Facebook and LinkedIn.

DAY 2
Publish a blog post with the video embedded in the blog post.

DAY 3
Post square promo video to Facebook, LinkedIn and/ or Instagram feeds.

DAY 7
Send out a newsletter that either links to your blog post or features the video.

DAY 10
Post the entire video to your Facebook, LinkedIn and/or IGTV.

DAY 14
Share a link to your blog post on Facebook and LinkedIn.

WHAT GOES WHERE?

Facebook

- Long form live videos
- Short form (1.5 - 3 minute) videos
- Teaser videos (<30 seconds)
- Videos for people in your network

YouTube

- Edited long form videos
- Any videos you plan to share on other social sites
- Videos you want found by people outside of your current audience

LinkedIn

- Videos that are engaging to a higher end audience
- Videos that show off your sales skills, offer a bit of educational information or include another professional

Instagram

- Videos that really catch the eye
- Short form videos (less than 60 seconds)
- Looking to reach locals outside of your network

Email

- Videos that are showing off a home to a warm audience
- Share as links to your YouTube videos that are less than 5 minutes long

Website

- Virtual Tour
- With your narration and introduction
- For people interested in that specific home

These worksheets can be downloaded at:

https://videoestateagent.com/book-downloadables/ and use the password: MoreViews.

Step 4: Create a Live Video Strategy

Try to go live at least twice a month. This could be on Facebook or Instagram or once on each, but live video is where the magic happens with clients. You don't have to go live for very long, but you should always schedule an hour for each live, in case there are potential technical difficulties or delayed responses from the audience.

Smart Tip: Pick two days a month where you block off one hour for live video.

Be prepared to be flexible. You may find that a virtual open house will be better for a specific listing. If that happens, just add another hour of live video to your calendar! The good news about live is that there is no post-production to worry about afterwards. Once it's done, it's done! All of the work is completed up front.

Ten Days Before: Schedule the live video on Facebook, post it to your website (if it's not for a listing, just make it an "Event" and create a short blog post for it).

Seven Days Before: Create a Facebook Event for it, share it on your Facebook Profile, mention it in your weekly newsletter.

Six to Two Days Before: Ask for questions in the Event discussion.

One Day Before: Talk about it in your Instagram Stories, post the Event to your Facebook Page and Profile again.

VIDEO MARKETING STRATEGY

7 - 10 DAYS BEFORE
Create a Facebook event for live virtual open houses

WEEK BEFORE
Foster engagement in your Facebook event DAILY

DAY 0
Post your full video (or go live) to your Facebook Page
Share your post to your Facebook Profile

DAY 1
Post full edited video to YouTube and MLS
Reach out to all people who attended live event

DAY 3
Post "preview" to Facebook (Page and Profile), LinkedIn and/or Instagram
Encourage people to view full video on YouTube
Send link to your email list

DAY 5
Put out a "teaser" video that has 1-2 clips in it on Facebook, Instagram, and/or LinkedIn

DAY 7 - 10
Post full video to Instagram and/or LinkedIn and follow up with all interested parties

Bonus Tip: Don't limit yourself to live video on social media. Live video can be done through Facetime or Zoom as well. Take the time to have these calls with clients. There are some things that are hard to explain over email or that need more of a personal touch than a phone call. For those topics, offer to do a video call. You will be surprised by how much of a difference it can make.

Step #5: Do it!

You just have to start. It's not going to be perfect. You're not going to hit the deadlines every single time. You will probably feel weird at first. But after you start to get the hang of it, video will become second nature. Soon, people are going to start complimenting you on your videos and they're going to start reaching out to you. Then they will trust you enough to hire you to help them buy or sell a home. So what are you waiting for? Lights. Camera. Close.

Conclusion

As we said at the beginning of this book, seeing is believing. As humans, we want to connect to someone by seeing their face, listening to them talk, and observing their mannerisms. These things help us understand each other's personalities and determine whether or not we click with one another. Videos make this possible, and there is no better way for you to create a trustworthy online brand than with videos that sell *YOU*.

As we hope we've demonstrated in this book, you have nothing to fear and nothing to lose from embracing video as a central real estate marketing strategy.

By now, you should have everything you need to plan, write, record, edit, post, and optimize your videos! You've learned why it's important to use video, how video helps you connect with others in a digital world, what sort of videos are most effective, and everything in between. Hopefully you feel more confident about seizing on this burgeoning marketing trend and using it to maintain and grow your business.

You are now well on your way to becoming a video star! Or, at least to attracting more clients, generating new leads, and embracing the future of real estate marketing. Be creative, be you, and have fun!

Lights! Camera! Action!

About the Authors

Brie E. Anderson is a seasoned digital marketer. She received her degree in Social Media Marketing from Western Kentucky University. During her college years, she had four internships - she was determined to learn as much as she possibly could. Before graduating, she secured a job at an agency in Wichita, Kansas, where she moved two weeks after graduation! At the agency, she was privileged enough to work with clients like the best franchise to buy (as named by Forbes), Freddy's Frozen Custard, one of the leading aviation companies in the world, Textron Aviation, the school she now teaches at, WSU Tech, and over 40 other clients. During this time, Brie handled over $500,000 in search engine optimization work, multiple social media campaigns and over $2 million in digital ad spend. Today, Brie is owner of BEAST Analytics, her digital marketing analytics and strategy consultancy.

Tracy Ramsay has been a Realtor® for over twenty years and was consistently in the top three percent of agents in her market. She maintains her real estate license, invests in income property, and is CCA-Certified Coach. She works as a sales/accountability coach for The Carnahan Group, Reece Nichols, South Central Kansas. Tracy has a Bachelor's Degree in Speech Communication Studies from Hamline University, Minnesota, and a Master's Degree in Communication from University of Northern Iowa. During graduate school, she taught in the speech communication department.

Claim Your Free Worksheets!

Go to the super-secret page, https://videoestateagent.com/book-downloadables/ and use the password: MoreViews

Download the worksheets by clicking the "download" buttons.

Create Your Persona

www.realestatepersonabuilder.com.

Enroll in a Video Estate Agent Course

Go to courses.videoestateagent.com and purchase the course best for you.

Find Video Estate Agent on Social Media

https://www.facebook.com/VideoEstateAgent

https://www.instagram.com/videoestateagent/

https://www.youtube.com/channel/UCcYnYXa-rTKrdELZ1p3489w

https://www.pinterest.com/videoestateagent/

ENDNOTES

[1] Maria, Jess. "45 Video Marketing Statistics." Video Marketing for Real Estate. October 15, 2013. https://www.virtuets.com/45-video-marketing-statistics/.

[2] Mansfield, Matt. "27 Video Marketing Statistics That Will Have You Hitting the Record Button." Small Business Trends. (Small Business Trends, May 26, 2020), https://smallbiztrends.com/2016/10/video-marketing-statistics.html.

[3] Savage, Jonathan. "Top 5 Facebook Video Statistics for 2016." Social Media Today. (Social Media Today, April 10, 2016), https://www.socialmediatoday.com/marketing/top-5-facebook-video-statistics-2016-infographic.

[4] Cisco. (2020). Retrieved from http://www.cisco.com/.

[5] National Association of Realtors®. (2020). Retrieved from https://www.nar.realtor/.

[6] Caron, David. "Video In Email Increase Open Rates & Reduce Unsubscribes," Video In Email Increase Open Rates & Reduce Unsubscribes | DCD Agency (DCD Agency, June 26, 2012), http://dcdagency.com/video-in-email-increase-open-rates-reduce-unsubscribes/.

[7] Royster, Kathryn. "Real Estate Video Marketing's Biggest Return on Investment: High-Quality Community and Listing Videos Syndicated to YouTube, Shared on Social," Inman, July 7, 2014, https://www.inman.com/next/by-the-numbers-how-to-focus-your-video-marketing-for-the-biggest-return-on-investment/.

[8] Royster, "Real Estate Video Marketing," Inman.

[9] Wong, Rachel. "A Realtors®® Guide to Video Marketing," RESAAS Blog (RESAAS, June 22, 2017), https://blog.resaas.com/articles/video-marketing-guide-for-Realtors®-infographic.

[10] Wong, "Realtors® Guide," RESAAS Blog.

Made in the USA
Middletown, DE
17 October 2022